SUPERSTUDY

John Wade

DELLASTA
Melbourne

To my children, Alexis and Sunny

They'll learn much more than I'll ever know,
And I think to myself, 'What a wonderful world!'

—Louis 'Satchmo' Armstrong

Dellasta Pty Ltd

© Edward John Wade

First published 1990

National Library of Australia
Cataloguing-in-Publication data:

Wade, Edward John
   Superstudy: a fresh approach to successful learning.

   ISBN 0 947138 60 9.

   1. Study, Method of. I. Title.

371.30281

Cover by Echidna Graphics
Text design by Ron Hampton
Typeset by Abb-typesetting Pty Ltd,
126 Oxford Street, Collingwood, Victoria 3066
Printed by Brown Prior Anderson Pty Ltd,
5 Evans Street, Burwood, Victoria 3125
Published by Dellasta Pty Ltd,
3/6 Hamilton Place, Mount Waverley, Victoria 3149
Correspondence to PO Box 777, Mount Waverley, Victoria 3149

Foreword

Education has undergone major changes in recent times. It was once the preserve of the wealthy, the remarkable and the lucky. Now few people have not done some secondary studies, and many have the opportunity to undertake post-secondary studies.

Education and travel have much in common. Not so long ago travel was restricted to the few who could afford the high cost. Mostly they were well prepared for this adventure—their parents had spoken fondly of their own experiences, so when they did travel, these young people felt at ease. Today, many people travel, but they tend to stay abroad only briefly and often do not integrate what they learn into their lives.

With society and the world of work now continually changing it is essential for everyone to undertake further study from time to time. It would be a pity if you felt as if you were in a foreign land, and could not make sense of the adventure!

Superstudy is a guide prepared by the expert educator John Wade from the personal experiences of successful learners. It orients readers to the basic processes of study and helps to identify styles of learning which are personally effective.

I particularly enjoy the new ideas that John has put forward in this work. In my many years of counselling and advising learners I have found that help is most often achieved by attention to basic processes. John has guaranteed this. By guiding you through a series of simple steps he helps you to incorporate profound resources into your learning strategies.

In presenting these from the perspective of the learner, from the inside out as it were, it is easy for you to incorporate them into your pursuit of excellence in learning. Even beyond that, it will add to your enjoyment of life itself. This book returns study to the realms of living!

I sincerely commend this book to both the serious and the curious students who wish to learn how to learn.

Marshall O'Brien
Director, Counselling Services
University of Canberra
1990

Acknowledgements

My appreciation goes to these people who have all personally contributed advice and encouragement to me during the writing of this book: Justin Belitz, Ahrara Bhakti, Walter Bellin, Glynn Braddy, Sigrid Gassner-Roberts, John Grinder, Michael Grinder, Karin Hannigan, Brian Haslem, Irene Hill, Frances Heussenstamm, Jean Houston, Eric Jensen, Zoltan Kelemen, Denise Linn, June Slatyer, Rona Wade, Lindsay Yeates.

The cartoons are by Richard Patterson and illustrations by Noeline Cassettari.

Contents

Preface

On the fringe of the Nullarbor Desert in Kalgoorlie, Western Australia, when Elvis was King, I failed high school. That was before I knew that anyone had a choice in the matter of passing or failing, or had a choice of scraping through or of becoming dux. I thought I was pretty dumb for a long time after I failed, until I discovered that scholastic and academic achievement is *all* the result of choice and technique.

Since then, developing and testing study techniques has been my continuing interest. It is an interest which has led me to discover a love of learning which I now have forever. I have gained a string of professional qualifications, and every so often I do another course just for the fun of it!

Although I started out as a builder's labourer and a storeman-packer, my interest eventually drew me into the field of formal learning. First I became a mature age correspondence student. Then I took up positions as a teacher, a university tutor, a head of department, then head of school, headmaster and finally as an educational adviser at primary, secondary and tertiary institutions in Australia and overseas. Highlights of my life were when Australian colleagues twice awarded me the status of Master Teacher—once in the primary-secondary school system and once in the technical and further education college system.

Through my demonstration classes many people have become familiar with work being done on neuropedia—which uses the brain's natural pathways of learning to make studying faster, easier and more effective for any students, no matter how badly or brilliantly they are performing at present—and as a result, articles, seminars and speaking appointments on accelerated learning reach widespread audiences. It is in response to requests from these audiences that *Superstudy* has been written.

Superstudy is a breakthrough from the old how-to-study books, with their messages of slog, slog, slog. It is practical, pragmatic and *fun*. Anyone consistently using these simple techniques holds the power to choose between passing or failing their courses of study. Are you ready to make the choice?

1 The Deep Mind and Pen-power

Your pen or pencil will help you get more out of this book than you would if you just read it through from cover to cover. You will be invited to pause from time to time and reflect on what you have just read—sometimes to make a contribution to it. Doing the exercises as you read through the book will enable you to understand their significance more readily. The ones that are important for you will stay in your memory without you having frequently to go back over the whole book.

Here is the first one. Find out for yourself how much you already know about efficiency in studying.

Take a minute to quickly jot down a list of seven or more things that you are already doing, or think you should be doing at present, to make your study or learning time as effective as possible (For example: When I feel happy). Follow the example below, and write whatever comes to mind. Write quickly, without analysing or thinking too much about it.

Study is efficient when:

1 I feel happy _____

2 _____

3 _____

4 _____

5 _____

6 _____

7 _____

Now look back over the list you have just made. You know some very powerful techniques, don't you? You probably already intuitively know the benefits of all the advanced techniques described in this book. The purpose of this book is to guide you to do your best in implementing them. When you do, your capacity to learn will be much greater than it is now. Your love of learning will also have begun.

The assumption here is that you do want to learn something or that you do want to pass an examination. Not all people want to be successful in their learning. Some people have a need to fail. Does this sound strange? Did you know that most people who fail do so not because of any intellectual disability but because they have a need to fail?

The need to fail

A lecturer tries to motivate new students by saying to them in their first lecture, 'Look to the person on your left. Now look to the person on your right. Only one of you will pass this unit.' His prophecy is correct. The failure rate is very high, even though all the students are intelligent enough to win a place in the course at the start of the year.

Take any group of students and you will find that there are Smart people and there are Plodders. Hardly any of the Plodders fail. Some of the Smarts get their high distinctions but many fail. Like the hare in 'The Hare and the Tortoise', the Smarts leave their run too late.

The strange thing is that the Smarts cannot see they are heading for failure. It is as though they have a need to fail, despite their obvious ability to pass. Why should this be so?

Consider that question for a few moments, and then, as before, jot down seven or more reasons without trying to analyse your thoughts.

Some people need to fail because:

1 _____

2 _____

3 _____

4 _____

5 _____

6 _____

7 _____

Sabotage from the deep mind

These reasons will be useful to you later. There are thousands of reasons why people need to fail. It is unfortunate for most people that the need is unconscious and is known only to the 'deep mind'. The deep mind is a part of you of which you are usually unaware. It is a strong force, and it works towards what it currently perceives to be your long-term satisfaction. It is the drive of the deep mind which causes people to fail. Here are some case histories.

- Steve failed his first year at university because it was a way of getting back at his father for forcing him to do a course he did not want to do. His deep mind solved that for him—it prevented him from concentrating. He had to choose another course—and he completed that with first-class honours! He still thinks he failed the first course because he was not clever enough.

- Lisa started to fail in her college subjects when her sister became a champion athlete. Everyone in her family was paying attention to her sister. Lisa felt she was being neglected. Her deep mind knew that she needed a fair share of love and attention from her parents; it knew she could get this by doing something that would earn the sympathy of the family. So she failed, and everyone was very sympathetic and thoughtful. Her deep mind got her what she wanted. She still thinks she was not clever enough to pass those subjects.

- Craig failed his university entrance exam because he took on a demanding job which exhausted his concentration at school and at home. His family had little money, and he believed he took the job to help out financially. What really happened was that if he had passsed his university entrance exam he would have taken on tertiary studies and would have remained financially dependent on the meagre resources of his family for three or four more years. His deep mind wanted him to be earning a salary to support himself and thus able to move away from the unhappy family environment in which he was presently enmeshed.

- Anne was an intelligent girl who was a scapegoat. Her family was one of those which needed one member to be 'dumb' so that all the others could feel more superior and more secure. Other family members would say to friends in front of her, 'Our Anne has never been too bright at school, have you dear?' By the time Anne reached the time to sit for the university entrance exam she thought she was a bit of a clot. She thought she hated study.

- Michelle was sailing though her law degree when she suddenly discovered how lawyers earned their money. She imagined herself as a glorified clerk, running around doing the dirty work for clients who did not have the courage to negotiate things for themselves. Who needs a law degree if all you get out of it is a career of wallowing in other people's conflicts, she wondered. Unless she can imagine a more inspirational work description than this, then the chances are great that she will fail, despite her best intentions and her abilities.

- Tristan's Year 12 friendship circle consisted of people who had no intention of gaining qualifications and who were only at school because it was less boring than being at home. Their friendship was important to him, and his deep mind was looking after his place in the group by causing him to fail. After all, if he performed to his full academic potential he would be a tall poppy, and they would cut him down to size by rejecting him from the group.

- Mary, at fifty-eight years of age, was brave enough to begin a university course for the first time in her life. Friends told her that learning was harder for older people. She started off enjoying her course, Linguistics, and achieved good marks. Halfway through the second year she was given a poor mark for one essay. 'Everyone is right. Studying is too hard for older people', she concluded, and dropped out, much to the disappointment of her lecturers. They had admired Mary because she was an intelligent student, as well as being a model for all the younger linguists. Mary failed to complete her course because she began to believe the pessimistic opinions of her friends, not because of any lack of ability.

People who fail courses rarely do so because of bad luck or because they are stupid. They fail because they need to fail. They have a lesson to learn from life which is more important than the lessons they are trying to study.

Have you ever failed anything? Yes? Then perhaps it had something to do with the reasons you listed above. When you jot things down quickly without analysing them, the power of your pen may be coming directly from your deep mind. Recheck your list, and see if anything jumps out at you—now that you have an understanding of what may be involved.

Are you worried about failing? If so, think about what could be happening in your life right now that would cause your deep mind to protect you by finding a way to stop you passing.

Go for success

Fortunately there is plenty you can do about it. If you suspect this may be happening to you, that is great! It is better to clear it up now than be worn out over a long period by the conflict between your conscious mind and your deep mind. Make an appointment to talk it over with a student counsellor. That is why your institution has a counsellor—to assist students having any sort of difficulties. Your counsellor will be delighted to have such an insightful person to talk to, and will be able to help you identify any conflict and to solve it. The counsellor's main job is to help you overcome difficulties which may interfere with your studies and passing your examinations.

Alternatively, sometimes talking it over with trusted friends or relatives will be enough to give you reassurance. Take care when you are seeking objective advice from your immediate family however—be aware of possibilities such as being a scapegoat and of fulfilling the family's needs rather than your own. If you choose to get really fired up for success, read the next chapter on affirmative action.

REVIEW

---

1 Do the exercises as you go through this book. Then you will not need to reread the whole book.

2 Examine anything you might unconsciously seek to gain by failing. Find another way to achieving it without having to fail. A counsellor can help.

---

2 Affirmative Action

Do you sometimes have thoughts like these?

I am stupid.
Everyone else is better than me.
Maths (or any other subject) is boring.
I hate studying.
My spelling (or any other skill) is terrible.
My essay marks are getting worse.
I will never finish my assignments on time.
Science (or any other subject) is difficult.
I have a bad memory.
I know I am going to fail.
I am unable to concentrate.
I will never be good enough.
I have a useless teacher.
Affirmative Action will not work for me.

There are many more, but now you have the general idea. Whenever you think something derogatory about your ability to deal with study you are programming your deep mind to increase that negative influence on you. Therapists call this self-talk, and it can be very powerful either when it is destructive, as in the above examples, or constructive.

Your deep mind also helps you to change your thoughts into reality. In doing this it uses a process similar to hypnosis. The hypnotherapist offers suggestions to the patient's deep mind. If the patient can imagine that these suggestions are beneficial, the deep mind accepts them and lends its power to make the suggestions become a new part of the patient's reality. For example, during hypnosis a smoker's deep mind may be asked to imagine the reality of how much better it feels to have stopped smoking, to exercise choice in looking after one's own health in a positive way; once more to know how sweet it is to breathe fresh air and to enjoy the taste of delicious food. If the deep mind approves these suggestions the patient is well on the way to becoming a non-smoker.

Self-talk can achieve similar ends without the necessity of going to a hypnotherapist. Whenever you notice than you have just had a deprecatory thought, first give yourself a pat on the back for spotting it, then simply think the opposite thought. Like this:

I am stupid → I am clever.
Everyone is better than me → I am as good as anyone else.

Maths is boring → Maths is interesting.
I hate studying → I love studying.
My spelling is terrible → My spelling is great.
My essay marks are getting worse → My essay marks are getting better.
I will never finish my assignments on time → I almost always finish my assignments on time.
Science is difficult → Science is easy.
I have a bad memory → I have a good memory.
I know I am going to fail → I pass my exams.
I am unable to concentrate → My concentration is fine.
I will never be good enough → I am good enough.
I have a useless teacher → My teacher is exactly the one I need to give me mastery of this subject.
Affirmative action will not work for me → Affirmative action works well for me.

Easy isn't it? Yet, at first, just thinking of the opposite may seem strange to you. Young people usually believe that most others are better than they are at learning. For some it may take years of enormous effort to even consider the remote chance that they are 'as good as anyone else'. It always seems like a terrible lie to them. As time passes they are confronted with little examples in life that provide proof that everyone has a vast range of different abilities and potential. Eventually they can begin to accept the possibility that the statement, 'I am as good as anyone else', is just as true as its opposite. When this happens they can release the limitations they have been putting on themselves, and start to live life more fully.

If you wish to start increasing your chances of success, immediately become alert to your self-talk, and when you find you are putting yourself down in any way at all get into the habit of using affirmative action.

Turbo boost

Affirmative action can be 'turbo-boosted' these days because a lot of work has been done in recent years to find the most effective ways of reaching the deep mind. Here are the boosted methods:

1   Reward yourself

    From now on, whenever you identify negative self-talk and turn it round into the equally true positive statement you will have empowered yourself by having more choices to act upon. This is excellent self-management, and deserves a reward. Eat a favourite food, or go and hug a tree, or do whatever you like to do to pat yourself on the back. Treat it seriously, and it will make a marvellous difference to you over the years.

2   Invert the statement

    Go overboard for a while—you have a lot of catching up to do; you have held the negative belief for a long time. Change 'I hate studying' to 'I love studying' even though at first it may grate.

3   Use positive language

The deep mind does not recognize negatives in speech. Use 'My spelling is very good' in preference to 'My spelling is not terrible' because the deep mind will interpret the latter as 'Spelling = Terrible', and will continue sabotaging your efforts to improve.

4   State it in the present tense

Use 'I am good enough' in preference to 'I will be good enough'. The latter is read by the deep mind as 'Sure. When pigs fly I will be good enough, but right now I can still use my insecurity to avoid tackling challenging things.'

5   Use the language of truth

Use 'I almost always finish my assignments on time' instead of 'I always finish my assignments on time' because the word 'always' is powerful, and there may be a time in the future when something vital may crop up which is more important than getting an assignment in on time. Inserting the word 'almost' will allow for this possibility while maintaining the truth of the affirmative action.

6   Personalize your affirmative action

Add your own name. Start with the statement in the first person, then put it into second and third person. Use your childhood first language if it was not English. Use your childhood name if it was different—unless it was a derogatory name such as 'Dumbo'.

'I cannot concentrate' becomes 'I concentrate well'
or 'I, Sparkie, concentrate well' (first person).

'You concentrate well, Sparkie' (second person).

'Sparkie concentrates well' (third person).

An explanation for why this is turbo-boosted lies in the fact that you have been subjected to negative programming in your early years by people using these forms of grammar when speaking to you: 'Oh, Sparkie, you can't concentrate for a minute, can you?' It helps to substitute life-affirming statements if you use similar grammar (in the second or third person).

As you become more practised you will be able to use voice tones from the past. Recreate the sounds of your parents or teachers when they were being critical, but this time have them being emphatically supportive of your positive qualities.

7   Activate affirmative action

(a)   Write affirmative action statements down. Use small cards and carry them in your wallet or purse so that you see them each time you get any money out. Write them on a small sheet of paper and stick it to your wall or your mirror. Fill a page in an exercise book with one every day for a week.

(b)   Say them and hear them. Record them onto one side of a C60 cassette. Repeat each one once every five to ten seconds for a total of about five minutes, and play them in the background as you are waking up and getting dressed in the morning. It is a happy way to start the day.

Kick start

Once you have identified negative self-talk, changed it for your affirmation, and begun affirmative action, it is time to use the kick start.

The kick start is used to get the engine of a motorbike going. Once your 'motor' is running, then affirmative action becomes your throttle or accelerator. After you start the 'motor' the affirmations accelerate your progress in the right direction without you having to think about restarting the motor all the time.

To use the kick start, simply do something (anything!) to corroborate in some way what you are telling yourself in the affirmation. For example, if you are using 'My spelling is terrific', kick start by practising the technique 'Excelling in Spelling', which is explained in Chapter 15. If you are working on 'Maths is interesting', kick start by using your imagination to find things when you do maths that are or could be interesting, and put a green tick near them in your book. If you are affirming your ability to concentrate, kick start by making a list of minute spans (5, 10, 15, ... 60). When you concentrate successfully for five minutes cross off the 5; when you do ten minutes cross off the 10, and so on.

Each affirmation has different opportunities for you to prove that what you are affirming is to some extent already true. Use the kick start to get your 'motor' going. Then sit back, open the throttle and enjoy the exhilaration of the ride.

Fast results

Use your affirmation constantly for just one week, then change it for a different affirmation. By the end of the second week you will probably have evidence of your affirmative action taking effect. For example, you will feel comfortable thinking to yourself 'I am clever', or more and more frequently you will be able to enjoy studying, etc.

If there is no change in your situation despite using the kick start, it is an indication that your deep mind objects strongly, and is not accepting the affirmation because it feels that it will be harmful for you to do so. You can discover and evaluate the objection, and then choose to discharge it, using the following technique.

The exposé

Rule a sheet of paper vertically in two. In the left column write the affirmation, and in the right column write your immediate reaction to it, like this:

Phrase	Instant Reaction
I'm clever	That's dumb.
I'm clever	Like a rock is clever.
I'm clever	How can I be? I failed science.
I'm clever	I'm good at getting laughs.
I'm clever	No one says I am.
I'm clever	Okay. I'm clever at some things.
I'm clever	—

At some point you will run out of thoughts to write down instantly after the affirmation. This is a sign that your deep mind has shown you somewhere in the instant reaction column why up until now it has rejected the affirmation. One of the reactions will seem slightly more significant to you than the others.

Suppose the one that stands out in the list you have written is 'Nobody says I am clever'. This may be true—perhaps nobody has specifically told you recently that you are clever. Your deep mind is operating on the premise that if nobody is telling you that you are clever, then you cannot be clever. Your conscious mind is aware of the flaw in this primitive pseudo-logic. However, respecting the power of the deep mind, you avoid inverting the statement directly to 'Everyone says I am clever' because this is not truthful, and will continue to be rejected. What you can do is to rephrase it to 'Everyone agrees that I am clever'. This could well be true. You can think of instances in your life when you have been clever enough to do something successfully and everyone would have had to agree.

Your next affirmation therefore becomes 'Everyone agrees that I am clever', which your deep mind will not reject. You can now relax, and watch your own esteem go up in the opinion of other people—a neat little bonus to your original affirmation of just learning to accept your potential cleverness.

Learning despite the teacher

What if the cause of your angst is beyond your control? Perhaps you have a bad teacher. How can you use affirmative action to solve this problem?

It is a wonderfully convenient excuse for a student to say, 'There is no point in doing any work in that subject. The teacher is useless. He does not like me and he would fail me anyway.' You would be rich if you had a dollar for every student in Australia who is using this old gem right now.

When graduates look back at their student days they realize that some of their most hopeless teachers were their best educators. Not that those lecturers taught well—they were thoroughly incompetent as teachers—the real lesson they taught was how to learn the subject in spite of the lessons. Their students developed self-sufficiency precisely because the lecturers communicated so badly. It forced those students to learn how to learn.

What to do

1   Go along to the lectures to get a rough idea of the areas they cover. Then find the relevant information in the library or elsewhere so that you can absorb it in a more digestible form. It may be more enjoyable learning it this way. There is more information on this in the section on 'Seers, Listeners and Doers' in Chapter 15.

2   At the same time as you are developing independence as a student, work on your relationship with each 'bad' lecturer. By the end of each course you might even feel genuine sadness when it is time to move on from their subjects. This requires a little further explanation.

   The qualities people dislike in others are similar to the qualities they dislike in themselves. They suppress these qualities from their conscious awareness because it is unpleasant for them to admit to themselves that these nasty or ugly tendencies are in their own psychological makeup. For example, imagine those people who react with self-righteous indignation when they find out others are cheating. The reason for their reaction is that somewhere in their psyche is a part that likes the thrill of a nefarious activity such as cheating. Because they suppress this 'ugly' part of their character they notice it acutely in other people. They loudly express their disapproval of cheating because this is how they got themselves liked by those around them. Rather than acknowledging the cheat in themselves, their deep minds project the bad quality onto any others they can find who also cheat. Ah, now they can be condemning because it does not hurt them, it only hurts the other people—the cheats.

   Here is how this knowledge can be of use:
   • Learn to identify why you dislike, criticize or blame the teacher, for example, 'She cannot explain things clearly'.

- Then recognize that this is a part of yourself that you do not like—'I cannot explain things clearly'—and that you have projected it onto the teacher.
- The next step is to commence affirmative action in order to change the deep-seated unconscious belief that is handicapping you. Your affirmation becomes 'I can explain things clearly'.
- Activate the affirmative action by any one of the means explained earlier, such as writing it down or recording it on a cassette.

By following these steps you can use your annoyance at 'bad' teachers to further the building of your own character.

Whitelighting

Since the bad teachers have been so helpful to you, it would be good to do something for the teachers in return. You can use an ancient technique for this; it is called 'whitelighting'.

Whenever you see the teachers or think of them, imagine them in a bubble of pure white light or sunlight. Then start mentally to list their good qualities—he dresses well, she finishes lessons on time, his sarcasm is witty, and so on.

When you do this regularly it is not long before you begin to notice a change in your relationship with them—a change for the better. You will become more aware that they are not too bad after all, and that just because they cannot teach is no reason to dislike them. The improvement in your personal relationships is valuable too, especially if they mark your tests and exams. They are more likely to award you better marks if you do not antagonize them.

This is a useful technique for anyone in your environment. It is too good to restrict its use to bad teachers. If you already have a good teacher and you want to move from a pass to a distinction, use whitelighting on this teacher too.

REVIEW

1 Reward yourself when you spot negative self-talk.

2 Invert the negative statements.

3 Use true, personal, positive, present-tense language.

4 Write or record the new statements.

5 Kick start.

6 If the results are slow do the exposé to release the sabotage of the deep mind.

7 Use affirmative action and whitelighting on ineffective teachers.

---

3 The Force Will Be with You

In institutional education it appears that the teaching and administrative staff have most of the power and the students have very little. This is true if you want it to be. It may thus be easier to blame the system or the teachers for anything that goes wrong. However, to be in a weak or 'victim' situation is not good for your academic progress. You will be pushed around, and ignored.

In order to realize your potential as a student, it is important to take full responsibility for your own learning. If you blame the system or the teachers, you are putting yourself in the role of a victim. You are saying that someone or something else is responsible for your progress or lack of it. This is false. All students are solely responsible for their own success, no matter what the circumstances. It helps no one, least of all the students, if they blame other people or events when things go wrong. If you are adopting the role of a victim you will say things like:

1 I can't come to training tomorrow.
2 I'd like to finish my assignment by Monday.
3 I'd like to get the book but it's too expensive.
4 I shouldn't have a beer before I finish studying.
5 I feel obliged to visit my friend in hospital.
6 I'll try to be clearer in my next essay.
7 This question is too difficult.
8 I should spend more time in the library.
9 I must get to bed by eleven o'clock.
10 I want to be more efficient in my study.
11 I hope to get a credit in biology this term.
12 I never argue with lecturing staff.
13 I always do my assignments on my own.
14 I need to show the lecturer that I studied hard.

Taking charge

It is simple to slip away from the victim role. All it takes is practice in recognizing when we are playing at being the victim, and then choosing to make the appropriate language substitution. Look at the above statements more closely, and find out how to take charge.

1 *I can't come to training tomorrow.*
  The implied meaning of this is that someone or something is preventing me from coming tomorrow. The truth is that I have decided that I

will not come to training tomorrow because I prefer to type my assignment, and this is more important to me than one training session. There is the possibility that I will be dropped from the team, and I have already considered this in making my decision. Whether or not I give my reason to the coach is up to me. The honest and responsible statement is therefore: 'I will not be coming to training tomorrow.'

2 *I'd like to finish my assignment by Monday.*
This implies that I might or might not do so. If I really want to finish it by Monday it is far more effective to make a commitment: 'I will finish my assignment by Monday' (come hell or high water).

3 *I'd like to get the book but it's too expensive.*
This implies that I will not get the book. If I want the book I make a commitment, 'I will get the book.' There are two words of weakness embedded in this statement that can be eliminated—'but' and 'too'. The statement now becomes: 'I will get the book. It's expensive.' This immediately opens up a range of possibilities as to how I can get the book. I can somehow find the money to buy it. I can find a way to get it more cheaply, I can borrow it, and so on. By rephrasing the statement, possession of the book is now within my power. I am no longer a victim.

4 *I shouldn't have a beer before I finish studying.*
This implies that someone or something is trying to stop me from having a beer. In truth the decision to have a beer is mine alone. Mindful of the consequences, I acknowledge my decisive power, and say: 'I won't have a beer before I've finished studying', or 'I will have a beer before I've finished studying'.

5 *I feel obliged to visit my friend in hospital.*
The implication is that some ethereal set of moral values out there is putting pressure on me to do something I may not really want to do. The truth is that either I want to visit him or I do not. The statements become: 'I will visit my friend in hospital', or 'I won't visit my friend in hospital'.

6 *I'll try to be clearer in my next essay.*
To try to do something is to imply failure. I am either trying to do something or I am doing it. I cannot be trying to do it and actually doing it at the same time. So instead of trying I will make a commitment: 'I will be clearer in my next essay'.

7 *This question is too difficult.*
Take charge by eliminating the 'too'. Then change the last word into 'challenging'. See what a difference it makes when you avoid giving your power away. Now it reads: 'This question is challenging'.

8 *I should spend more time in the library.*
Who is stopping me? No one. 'I will organize right now to spend more time in the library.'

9 *I must get to bed by eleven o'clock.*
Who says so? Nobody. It is my own choice, so that is how I say it: 'I choose to get to bed by eleven o'clock.'

10 *I want to be more efficient in my study.*
This is an interesting one. The truth is that I already have the capacity to be as highly efficient as anyone else. If I stop for a moment I will think of examples in my life when I have been efficient at doing something. I can transfer this efficiency to my study by using an affirmative action statement and acknowledging to myself that 'I am very efficient in my study.'

11 *I hope to get a credit in biology this term.*
Hoping implies the possibility that somehow the cosmos could intervene to thwart my aspirations. By now I am aware that if I decide to get a credit in biology that is exactly what I will do. My statement is: 'I will get a credit in biology this term.'

12 *I never argue with lecturing staff.*
The word 'never' weakens me because it restricts my options. Although at present I may think it is survival strategy to avoid conflict

with lecturers, conceivably there could be a time when a good show-down with a lecturer would be quite beneficial. To keep this option open, I substitute the word 'rarely': 'I rarely argue with lecturing staff.'

13   *I always do my assignments on time.*
The word 'always' is just as limiting as the previous example. Change it to 'nearly always' or 'usually': 'I nearly always do my assignments on time.'

14   *I need to show the lecturer that I studied hard.*
To have a 'need' is like having an external or internal force, using 'me' to find satisfaction for it. When I use this word I am giving away some of the power of 'me'. Who needs this? Not me. The honest and empowering statement once again is: 'I will show the lecturer that I studied hard.'

Keep it to yourself at first

You are now aware that by using responsible language and by avoiding the language of excuses you can summon up more of your own personal power. The more often you call on your own power, the more power you develop within yourself.

Becoming aware of the power latent within yourself can be a scary experience until you get used to the idea. Be happy at first just to observe yourself giving away your power from time to time. When you can do that, the next step is to make the correction by saying the responsible statement silently to yourself. Finally, when you are confident enough of your own worth, you can say the empowering statement, whenever, wherever, and to whomever you want.

Pen practice

Enjoy a preview of the sort of fun you can have with this technique as you develop it. Just ponder on any of the situations you are involved in at present, regardless of how big or small they are. Ask yourself if there is any way you can exert your own power more strongly. As you think of a way, complete your own list of the following:

1   I will _____

2   I choose to _____

3   I rarely _____

4   I nearly always _____

5   _____ is challenging.

6   _____

   and _____

REVIEW

Empower yourself by using	*Avoid*
I will . . .	I'd like to . . .
I choose to . . .	I should/shouldn't . . .
almost always	always
rarely	never
and	too
	but
	I'll try to . . .
	I must/mustn't . . .
	I hope to . . .
	I can't . . .

4 Targeting: Taking Control of Your Future

One of the main causes of mental exhaustion is when your conscious mind is heading in one direction and your deep mind is heading in another. When both are aligned you have a lot more energy, you enjoy what you are doing, the task you are working on is interesting (whatever it is), you can concentrate for long periods and you feel pretty good all over.

While the deep mind is more interested in long-term goals ('I am getting myself down to normal weight'), the conscious is often preoccupied with short-term goals ('I must have one of those hot doughnuts now'). However, it is easy to satisfy both concurrently. By doing a simple exercise you can find out which way your deep mind would prefer to move in the future.

The process takes only a few minutes. Programme it into your diary to do every seventh week. Do it now, just by reading straight from the book. Later you can read it onto a cassette, so that you do not have to find it in the book every seventh week.

The instructions are easy to remember. Read it through once, and then close your eyes. Open your eyes to peek whenever you want to.

The guide within

1   Close your eyes.

2   Take, and release slowly, a couple of very deep breaths.

3   Imagine you are pleasantly comfortable. Pretend you are watching a relaxing show on television. You do not have to actually see any particular show in your mind's eye, just get the relaxed feeling.

4   Now imagine there is pause in the television show and a commercial comes on. It seems to be coming from the future about a century from now. In the commercial there is the strong, happy, wonderful, human figure of a sage. It is easy to see that the figure has lived life to the full. Satisfaction and wisdom are radiating from the person. As you move closer you notice that the figure looks familiar. In fact, it is you in many years' time.

5   Ask the sage your question, 'What is my life purpose?'

6   The figure is delighted in your interest and soon starts to reply, so just sit still for a while and wait for the answer to come into your imagination.

7   After a few moments thank the figure for being there, and then open your eyes and take a couple of deep breaths.

8   Write down the answer.

Life purpose

The answer may come in any number of forms. You may imagine that you hear the figure talking, having a conversation, making a statement, or setting a question for you to answer. Or you may see the figure change into something else. A strange sign or symbol may pop into your head. Sometimes you will think of a new idea and then notice how good your body starts to feel—this means that the idea is an important one for your future. You might imagine a wonderful scent or aroma, or even a taste. Any, or all, of these will mean something to you. If the meaning is not immediately obvious, use 'embodiment' to pretend to become the image, and you will better be able to understand your direction. See Chapter 14 for instructions on the technique of embodiment. The images you receive can give strong indications regarding the future goals you could successfully choose.

Most people get something the first time they do this exercise, but it may be that initially you do not get an answer in any form that is obvious enough to write down. That is because the figure needs a little time to search for the answer, just as a computer needs a little time to search for the information requested of it. Be vigilant, however, for it can come into your mind when you are least expecting it! You may have a dream that contains the answer; you may notice a sign or symbol coming into your thoughts from time to time; you may hear an identical comment in several completely different contexts. Whichever way the answer comes, record it with your pen as soon as you notice it.

The sage who is delighted in your interest is not really you as a centenarian of course. It is your deep mind which is able to communicate to you openly through this exercise.

Expanding yourself

It is not necessary to rely totally on 'the guide within' to provide all your goals. It is easy to identify other long-term ambitions that do not bring you into conflict with the deep mind. These are goals or targets that you feel good or excited about as you are writing them down. They can come in many different categories. Here are some examples.

Education
What qualifications would you like to have that you do not have yet?

Skills
What would you like to be able to do that you cannot do yet?

Vocation
Where is your ideal place in the work force?

Family

What would you like to improve in your family relationships?

Personal communication

What would you like to change about the way you relate to people in general?

Friendships

Are you comfortable in your relationships with your current friends or do you want to choose others?

Intimacy

In what ways could you improve your intimate relationships?

Leisure

How can you get time to do what you really want to do, and to enjoy what you really want to enjoy?

Health

What can you do to improve or maintain your levels of health, fitness and nutrition?

Wealth

Do you have enough money now? How much would you like to have in the future?

Appearance

Are you happy with your clothes, your hair-style, your teeth? Is there anything you would like to improve?

There are also other areas that would benefit from your attention, but only a few are relevant to you right now. In your case, you are reading this book to develop more ability in your study programme. Be aware that your success in study is linked to the other areas of your life as well, so include different categories whenever you feel the desire to do so.

Stepping stones

Keeping contact with 'the guide within' for your lifetime goals, you can now break them down into more manageable time frames. Sets of seven are convenient: seven-year targets, seven-month targets, seven-week targets, and seven-day targets. Spend a little time on this list every seventh week.

Celina's targeting

Here is the targeting from the diary of a student, Celina:

> *My Life Purpose*
> Two symbols came to me. In the first an eye is the centre of an outwardly ever-expanding spiral. In the second is the outline of my body with rays of energy radiating outwardly from my heart and from my right hand.

My interpretation of the first is that my life purpose is to crystallize the experiences I have had and the things I have seen with my inner eye over the years. The outward spiral means that I must share these experiences with more and more people.

The second symbol means to me that this sharing must come from my heart (personal experience, not merely a collection of other people's intellectual theories), and through my hand (writing this diary is a way of expressing through my hand).

Then she wrote down her seven-year targets. As she thought of them she checked to see that they were generally compatible with her life purpose. If she felt uneasy about a seven-year target she put a question mark next to it to show that it could be in conflict with her life purpose.

My Seven-year Targets
1 To be satisfied that I have done everything possible to help my children become capable confident adults.

2 To return for a visit to my homeland in South America.

3 To be self-employed in interesting work where I can use my hands (to create) and my heart (to express myself).

4 To have a six-figure yearly income.

5 To be healthier and have even more vitality than I have now.

6 To have a wider circle of close friends.

7 To be learning something totally different from anything I know now.

These are sample seven-year targets from Celina. It is your turn now. Your list will be very different. First go back to the section 'The guide within', and see what communication you obtained, if any. If you have your life purpose worked out already, write it down first, and keep it in mind as you jot down your seven-year targets.

Life purpose

_____

_____

_____

_____

_____

_____

You can really be imaginative with your seven-year targets. Why settle for backpacking in Bali when you could aim at going right through Asia, or visiting all the seven continents? Why go for a job as a journalist when you could be the owner–publisher of your own national magazine?

While you are writing down each of the seven-year targets, keep tuned into your body. You may notice either a good feeling or an apprehensive one in your body. This is your deep mind agreeing or disagreeing with the target. Put a question mark after the targets that spark off a little apprehension.

Seven-year targets

1 _____

2 _____

3 _____

4 _____

5 _____

6 _____

7 _____

When this is done, look at which of the seven-year targets seem to be more urgent or easier to achieve than others. Keep these in mind as you write down the seven-month targets. Here are Celina's as examples:

My Seven-month Targets
1 To play regular ball games with my children. (One of them brought home a report last term that says they think fielding means 'getting out of the way of the ball').

2 To teach my kids something from *Superstudy*.

3 To have saved three hundred dollars in my travel account.

4 To be using all relevant parts of *Superstudy*, including nutrition and the warm-up.

5 To have successfully completed my diploma.

6 To talk to at least one self-employed person every month to find out how they got into business (hairdresser, electrician, newsagent).

7 To have three holiday weekends totally free of study.

Your turn again. You have the idea now. Take the urgent or important ones out of your seven-year list and break them down into seven-month targets. Add whatever others you like.

Repeat the steps with the seven-week and the seven-day targets. Do it with a sense of fun!

Seven-month targets

1 _____

2 _____

3 _____

4 _____

5 _____

6 _____

7 _____

Seven-week targets
(This is the best way to plan revision for exams)

1 _____

2 _____

3 _____

4 _____

5 _____

6 _____

7 _____

Seven-day targets

1 _____

2 _____

3 _____

4 _____

5 _____

6 _____

7 _____

If this is the first time you have ever written down targets you will notice that just by doing this you are much more in control of your life, especially of your studies. Your goals are different from Celina's because they reflect your own study programmes. For example, your seven-week targets could be something like this:

1 Finish draft of Assignment 3.

2 Read up to ch. 5 of Renton & Thomas.

3 Finish interviews for psych. survey.

4 Prepare for seminar on 26th.

5 Throw a winter solstice party.

6 Get info re career opportunities in BHP.

7 Visit Grandad.

Imagine in this example that you had a slightly uneasy feeling about number 6. If so, you would toss it around for a while before acting on it, look for a more suitable alternative, or even drop it completely.

You can adapt the time-scale to suit your own preference. Some students prefer this scale:

Life purpose
Five-year targets
One-year targets
One-term targets
One-week targets.

Getting the targets on paper, no matter what the time scale, is an instant cure for those times when you feel that control of your life is too much out of your hands.

Directional aids

A navigator repeatedly checks directional aids to ensure that the aircraft is proceeding towards its destination. Like the navigator, keep monitoring your progress and focusing on your targets. Keep them in view by sticking them up on the wall ('Blutack' is recommended—it doesn't mark the wall!). Sometimes students like Celina use a more flowing style, or perhaps add some colour to the list by writing in coloured felt-tipped pens.

Notice that Celina has drawn in lines to bring related goals together. This shows her where directions are integrating, and are therefore more likely to be satisfying. Seven-day targets are written directly into her daily diary every Friday.

Because she does the whole process regularly it now takes her only about seven minutes every seven weeks. That is just over an hour a year—well worth the time.

More often than not these days her deep mind is eager to help out. A day or two before she plans to do the seventh week 'guide within' exercise, symbols or messages about her life purpose start coming to her, so she does not have to sit down and do that part of the sequence. After jotting down the life purpose, she can start straight away with the seven-year targets.

Every seventh week you can take down the old sheet from the wall, and file it. Occasionally look back over the file to see how you are progressing. Sometimes some of the targets change completely—at any of the different time levels. This is a signal that you no longer have to develop in that area at this time. With hindsight you will see that you needed to do some of those things then. It was necessary then because in doing them you have learned the skills that enable you to tackle the challenges in life that are now before you.

A survey was carried out in the USA by researchers who interviewed students to see whether or not they were recording their goals. The same people were interviewed a few years later when they were in the workforce. The findings showed that the majority of people who had written out their targets as students had achieved them. Even those who had not achieved their precise goals had been more successful in their professions than those people who had never kept written goals as students. The lesson is to find

LIFE PURPOSE- CELINA

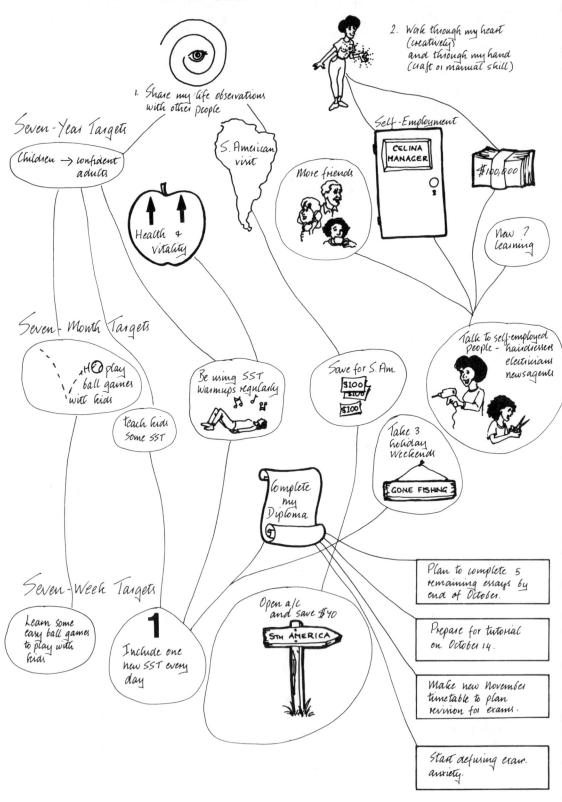

1. Share my life observations with other people

2. Work through my heart (creatively) and through my hand (craft or manual skill)

Self-Employment

CELINA MANAGER

$100,000

Seven-Year Targets

Children → confident adults

Health & Vitality

S. American visit

More friends

New ? learning

Seven-Month Targets

H play ball games with kids

Teach kids some SST

Be using SST Warmups regularly

Save for S. Am. $100 $100 $100

Talk to self-employed people - hairdressers electricians newsagents

Take 3 holiday weekends

GONE FISHING

Complete my Diploma

Seven-Week Targets

Learn some easy ball games to play with kids

1 Include one new SST every day

Open a/c and save $40

STH AMERICA

Plan to complete 5 remaining essays by end of October.

Prepare for tutorial on October 14.

Make new November timetable to plan revision for exams.

Start defusing exam. anxiety.

your goals, and to write them down. Chalk up another point to the power of the pen.

REVIEW

1 Use 'The guide within' to find your current life purpose.

2 Expand yourself to target:
education
skills
vocation
family
intimate relationships
friendships
leisure
health
wealth
appearance.

3 Every seventh week write down your life purpose, seven-year targets, seven-month targets, and seven-week targets.

4 Use your diary to record seven-day targets, and display all other targets on your wall.

5   Studying Is an Easy Job

If you are a full-time student it is useful to think about what you would be doing if you were not studying. You would probably be working or on the dole. The dole is an unsatisfying way to exist, so let us suppose that you would have a full-time job. That would involve about 40 hours a week of your time, for a minimal salary. Your salary would gradually increase, but unless you were exceptionally successful your life earnings would be only around half those of the average graduates, even though graduates do not start earning until after they have completed their courses.

Full-time study may seem an onerous load for a student, but when compared to a full-time job there is not much difference except that the study is likely to be more interesting than a job. Workers get paid, of course, but students will more than make up for this when they do start earning, even with the graduate tax. It is reasonable, therefore, to allocate to study the same number of hours each week as workers would complete—about 40 hours a week.

If you are prepared to commit yourself to 40 hours of quality study each week your chances of failing are miniscule because the educational institutions plan their courses exactly that way. That is, they assume that the average students will apply themselves for 40 hours a week on a regular basis.

As an example, if four units are considered a full-time load, then each will be planned to take the average student 10 hours to cover. If three units constitute the full-time course, each unit is planned to take about 13 hours to cover. This allocation includes time taken up by lessons, lectures and tutorials, as well as studying time. It does not include travelling time, coffee breaks, sports time, or any of the other fringes of full-time educational life.

With these parameters you can now make a formula on which to base the correct amount of study time. Imagine students who have 18 hours a week of lectures and tutorials. The formula would be:

Time spent in lectures and tutorials	18 hours
Study time (to make up to forty hours)	22 hours
Total time spent on formal learning	40 hours

which is the same time they would spend on a job. The students could expect to spend 22 hours each week on study.

Compulsory fun

The only thing that needs to be added to the formula is time spent on compulsory fun or leisure, such as socializing, entertainment, exercise or sport. This is a vital part of a realistic study programme. It is essential to incorporate leisure into your study programme, preferably in the ratio of learning:leisure of 4:1.

The purpose of leisure is to allow the part of your mind that understands and remembers information to catch up to the part of your mind that analyses and processes new information. If this does not happen you will suffer from information overload. When this occurs it becomes impossible to concentrate on lectures, and the mere thought of sitting down to study completely jams your mind. The learning:leisure ratio of 4:1 is a rule of thumb; however, most people find this to be the right amount of time to set aside for compulsory fun.

Continuing with our example, the time to be allocated in the timetable now comprises:

Lectures and tutorials	18 hours
Other study time	22 hours
Sub-total	40 hours
Compulsory fun	10 hours
Total time to be timetabled	50 hours

How to organize 30 spare hours every week

The composition of a timetable is a very personal thing, so the one presented here has to be hypothetical. The four main study slots are:

1 Before breakfast.

2 Between breakfast and lunch.

3 Between lunch and dinner.

4 After dinner.

You might timetable 50 hours like this:

	Sun	Mon	Tues	Wed	Thurs	Fri	Sat
		⟨½⟩	⟨½⟩	⟨½⟩	⟨½⟩		
	B R	E	A	K	F	A	S T
	③	③	③	③	③	②	
		L	U	N	C	H	
		②	③	②	③	②	
	D	I	N	N	E	R	
		③	③	③	②	⟨4⟩	⟨4⟩

KEY	⟨½⟩ Compulsory leisure	= 10 hours each week
	② Study	= 22 hours each week
	③ Lectures	= 18 hours each week

Notice that there are no specific times written on this table. That allows for a bit of leeway, in that it is only necessary to do, say, three hours of study between lunch and dinner on Thursday. Whether it is from 1–4 p.m. or 2–5 p.m. or 1–2 p.m. and 4–6 p.m. does not matter as long as the full three hours are done.

Likewise, in the above example if it is raining on Wednesday morning, you may decide to postpone a breakfast jog until Wednesday afternoon or Friday or Saturday morning.

At first glance the timetable seems rigid, but in fact it is quite flexible. Within each week you can move your blocks of study/leisure around. If you get an invitation to a party on Wednesday night, accept. Just re-slot that study time to another part of the week. There is plenty of alternative time—more than 30 hours. The timetable lists 50 hours of learning/leisure. Let us assume you plan for 8 hours of sleep every night. Then add 4 hours daily for miscellaneous activities, such as cooking, eating, cleaning, shopping, and commuting. That gives you:

Learning and leisure	50 hours
Sleeping (8 hours × 7 days)	56 hours
Miscellaneous (4 hours × 7 days)	28 hours
Total time used so far	134 hours

Now, each week has 24 hours × 7 days, or 168 hours. Thus 168 hours minus 134 hours leaves 34 hours of free time. So there is a reservoir of over 30 hours each week for you to draw on if the timetable is occasionally disturbed.

Part-time students

It is important for part-time students or business people to plan a timetable carefully, and stick to it. Use a modification of the example timetable above. Leisure is just as crucial for you to plan so that the after-work learning ratio is still 4:1. Flexi-timetabling could be especially useful to you as a part-time student.

Flexi-timetabling

A small percentage of people find the above style of timetabling does not work very well for them, it is a struggle to switch their concentration on and off according to the demands of their timetable. They are the students who may sleep in all Monday morning, then get up and go to their Monday afternoon lecture and later study with good concentration for seven or eight hours straight. If you recognize yourself as having this pattern, the flexi-timetable could be more suitable for you. Like the one we looked at above, it is a matter of calculating the time spent in lectures and tutorials, adding the hours of study time necessary to make up the 40 hours, and adding 10 hours of compulsory fun.

In your diary, record the precise tally of quality time spent at study or lessons. For example, if you are in the library from 9 a.m. to 9 p.m. but spend a few hours on coffee and meals, a few hours chatting to friends, and some time reading today's newspapers, you may only end up doing 4 hours of effective study. So only 4 hours are recorded.

There are advantages in the flexi-timetable. It is possible to get enthusiastic about an assignment, and work long, hard and well on it. In one week perhaps 70 hours could be spent on study. Then, just like flexitime in the public service, after a couple of weeks of extra work a credit of hours is built up until you earn a guilt-free long weekend of complete rest and recreation.

Flexi-timetabling works best when more time is allocated to weaker units of study. Remember to include the element of compulsory fun.

WEEK	10 20 30 40 50 60 70 80 90 100 hours	RUNNING TOTAL
1	−1	−1
2	−7	−8
3	+12	+4
4	+15	+19
5	−20	−1

This student completed 49 hours of study/lessons in Week 1, leaving a debit of 1 hour. During Week 2 the student subtracted 7 hours, increasing the debit to 8 hours. Week 3 was a good one, with 12 extra hours, bringing the running total to a credit of 4 hours. Week 4 added 15 hours to build the credit up to 19. Week 5 was the payoff—only 30 hours of study/lessons were completed because Friday, Saturday and Sunday were spent at a holiday shack.

You might like to do one of these graphs for each of your units of study or leisure, as well as for the weekly combined tally. That will give you an exact picture of how much time is being allocated to each unit, and allows you to see at a glance whether adequate time is being spent on the weaker subjects.

Some students use both the traditional timetable and the flexi-timetable concurrently. Charting progress through the course, week by week, in this way reassures the students that they are doing enough work to pass all units. These students never need to join the queues at the university health centre to ask for anti-anxiety medication as many of their fellow students do in the last few weeks of their courses. Their simple graphs tell them they will pass.

Pen-power time again

Take a pen and a sheet of paper, and use the next ten minutes to draw up your own personal weekly timetable.

The case of the missing days

Some people are able to draw up a timetable and put it to use immediately. However, when Justin, a college student, asked me to check his first timetable, something was wrong. It seemed fine, but he said that by the end of each week he was short by a couple of days. He could only fit in 30 hours when the timetable showed he should have done 40.

I suggested that he carry a mini-notebook for three consecutive days, and carefully record everything he did, and how many minutes it took to do each thing. A few days later he returned. His first day looked like this

Thursday

Activity	Minutes	Total
Sleeping	450	450
Shower, loo, etc.	22 + 5 + 3 + 3	33
Jog	50	50
Breakfast	30	30
Commute to/from uni	20 + 20	40
Pre-study exercises	9 + 9 + 9	27
Study sessions	120 + 95 + 95	310
Tea/coffee breaks	40 + 95 + 50	135
Lecture	60	60
Meditation	20	20
Tutorial	60	60
Lunch	55	55
Phone calls	10 + 45	55
Supermarket	55	55
TV + dinner (together)	60	60
TOTAL		1440

It became obvious to him that too much time was being spent on tea breaks, phone calls, shopping and several other areas. He did not want to cut these things out completely because they were important to him. Instead he trimmed them down to a reasonable amount of time so that he did not have to rush, and could still get almost as much satisfaction out of them.

He decided to be more assertive when it was time to finish a phone call or a coffee break. As far as I know, he never offended anyone by doing this—he simply told them he wanted to get on with other matters. Next time I saw him he reported feeling better whenever he remembered to do that. He said his timetable was a whole seven days long again, and it was easier to follow accurately.

REVIEW

1 Full-time students work a 40-hour week.

2 Plan for 20 per cent of compulsory fun (a ratio of 4:1).

3 Timetable for 50 hours study and leisure a week.

4 Use the flexi-timetable alternative for guilt-free weekends off.

5 Do the three-day time budget to avoid time wastage.

---

6 Maximum Power to the Study Session

The twin engines of the brain

When you see lamb brains at the butcher's shop you see the outside surface, which is called the neocortex. Beneath this there are other layers. In humans the neocortex is the largest part of the brain. The neocortex is in two parts, side by side. Imagine two lamb brains, side by side, weighing a total of 1.3 kilograms and you have a picture of a human brain, seven-eighths of which is neocortex.

The two parts are called hemispheres: the left hemisphere is on the same side of the brain as the left shoulder and the right hemisphere is on the side of the right shoulder. If you are not a specialist both sides might appear to be a mirror image of each other. Even though they are so similar in size, shape and weight, each of the hemispheres dominates the other in almost all functions.

For most people the functions are divided like this

Left brain	Right brain
logic	intuition
fact	fantasy
sequence	simultaneity
lists	patterns
details	wholes
languages	pictures, feelings
analysis	synthesis
rationality	metaphor
convergence	divergence
abstraction	concreteness

Hemispheric dominance is like hand dominance. Except for the rare person who is truly ambidextrous, every person prefers to use one hand in preference to the other. Most people prefer their right hand to their left. This does not mean that the left hand is never used—only that it is used less than the right. So it is with hemispheric dominance.

Because speech is a left-brain function it does not mean that the right brain has nothing to do with language. If the language area of the left brain is destroyed, the person might learn to speak again using the right brain. So it is with all functions. There are cases where a complete hemisphere has been surgically removed and the remaining hemisphere has taken over all of the functions of the missing hemisphere. In other words, both hemispheres have the potential for being able to perform any function.

There is an evolutionary explanation for the dominance of one side over the other. It is more efficient for the organism to evolve in this way. It is more efficient for one hand to be highly developed and the other hand to be an assistant than it is for both hands to be equally highly skilled. Similarly with all the dual parts of our bodies, such as the eyes, ears, arms and legs, one of the pair is almost always dominant.

Left or right: which are you?

Time for a bit of physical action. These exercises will demonstrate to you that one or other hemisphere is dominant for each example.

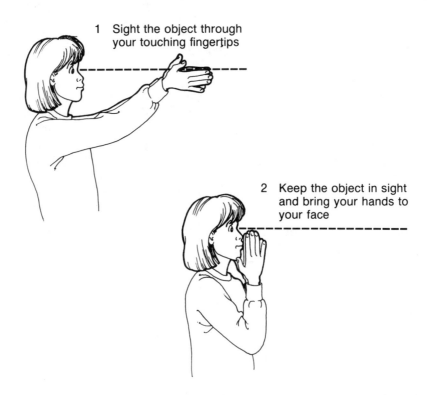

1 Sight the object through your touching fingertips

2 Keep the object in sight and bring your hands to your face

Eyes

With both eyes open extend your arms straight out in front, palms flat together as if you were going to dive or pray.

Keep both eyes open, and line up a distant object with your fingertips as if the fingertips were a gunsight.

With both eyes continually focused on the object keep your fingertips in line as you bring your hands slowly to your face.

When your hands reach your face the fingertips are closer to one eye or the other. This is your dominant eye.

The opposite hemisphere dominates its functioning.

Tick (or write down) your eye-dominant hemisphere:

Left ☐   *Right* ☐

Ears

In the mirror, note which of your ears is slightly higher or larger.

Do you always put the same ear to every telephone you use?

Which ear do you crane forward when you strain to hear a faint noise?

The opposite hemisphere controls it.

Tick (or write down) your ear-dominant hemisphere:

Left ☐   *Right* ☐

Hands

Which hand do you write with?

The opposite hemisphere probably controls it. However, if you started life as a natural left-hander and were forced to change to the right hand, your left hemisphere may still be dominant. How do you usually hold a pen in your right hand when you write? Does it point towards the bottom of the page and not to the top of the page? If so, you are naturally left-handed even though you use your right hand. If you are naturally left-handed, then your right hemisphere is dominant.

Tick (or write down) your hand-dominant hemisphere:

Left ☐   *Right* ☐

Legs

When you tip over stones or bits of wood with your feet to see if there are any spiders underneath, which foot do you use? When you are angry, which foot do you kick the wall with? Which foot kicks the football? Which foot kicks the car tyre of the used car you are thinking of buying? Which foot is a fraction longer or larger?

The opposite hemisphere is dominant.

Tick (or write down) your leg-dominant hemisphere:

Left ☐   *Right* ☐

Face

Hold a sheet of paper vertically at right angles to your face so that the middle of one of its sides touches your nose. Look in the mirror, and you will see the left side of your face on one side and the right side of your face on the other side. Which is larger? Estimate this by closing one eye at a time.

The hemisphere opposite the larger side is dominant.

Tick (or write down) your face-dominant hemisphere:

Left □   Right □

It is rare for anyone to score consistently left or consistently right. Most people will tend to one side or the other. Your results allow you to see for yourself some of the dominance functions of your brain.

Your dominant hemisphere

From the brain functions listed earlier you can see that most people who operate more frequently out of their left brain are good at logical, linear, detailed, analytical work. If the left brain is too dominant the person may become heavily intellectual. People like this are often in an emotional mess because they cannot envisage far enough into the future to establish their life purpose. Perhaps they are not even aware of how they are feeling most of the time. Left-brain-dominant people see the trees but not the forest. They see how useful trees are, and keep hacking into them, one after the other, until the forest has gone.

Those who operate mainly out of their right brain are better at intuitive, creative, holistic, synthesizing work. Too far into this side, and you become a dreamer who sees visions of how wonderful things can be in the future— but, as for doing anything about it (yawn), what a bore!

Can you recognize yourself already as leaning towards one of these sides or the other? Check the list of left- and right-brain functions given earlier to see which things you feel at home with.

Here is another way you can discover whether you are left- or right-brain-dominant.

The Plumb-bob

A plumb-bob is any sort of pendulum, such as a pendant on a necklace or a key on a keychain. The chain or string must be 20 centimetres, or longer.

Without resting your arm on anything, dangle the plumb-bob so that the weight is close to the surface of your desk or table. Hold the plumb-bob as still as possible, and start saying or thinking, 'Yes, yes, yes, yes, yes' continuously, until the weight starts to move. Its movement may be clockwise or anticlockwise, side to side, or forward and backward. It is important that you do not try to do this consciously, just let it happen of its own accord. When you get a steady movement in a set direction this becomes your 'Yes' response.

Put the plumb-bob down for a moment, rest your arm for a little while, and then repeat the dangling process while you are saying or thinking, 'No, no, no, no, no', continuously, as before. When you get a consistent move-

ment which is different from the 'Yes' movement, that is your 'No' response.

Check out both the 'Yes' response and the 'No' responses again to make sure the different movements are repeated for each response.

You now have an extremely valuable tool. It gives you direct access to the opinion of your deep mind. If ever you wish to consult your deep mind when making any great decision, use the plumb-bob to find the answer. Doing this will avoid any anxiety that may have been set up by a conflict between your conscious and your deep mind.

Knowing the potential of the plumb-bob, it seems trite to use it for such a simple thing as finding out which of our brain hemispheres is dominant. The beauty of it, however, is that it answers all questions with equal sincerity, as long as it only has to answer 'Yes' or 'No'. You can put to it, 'It is okay for me to have a Mars Bar now', or 'I should change my course from Arts to Law', and both answers will be equally valid. You can get quite detailed information from the plumb-bob if you address your questions to it in the correct sequence. Here is an example.

Suppose you have a feeling that you should change your course from Arts to Law but you are terrified that it could be a monumental blunder. You could proceed this way:

> Changing from Arts to Law is in my best interests. *Yes*
> (If you get a 'No', accept it. If your strong feeling about changing comes back later, use the plumb-bob again when next you are doing your seven-weekly targeting.)
> Changing from Arts to Law immediately is best for me. *No*
> Completing the Arts degree before changing is best. *No*
> Next year is the best time to change from Arts to Law. *No*
> Next semester is the best time to change. *Yes*

Is there anything else I need to consider?	*Yes*
Is it my finances?	*No*
Is it my accommodation?	*Yes*
Moving out of the group house is best for me.	*Yes*
Moving into a uni. hall of residence is best.	*No*
Returning to live with my parents is best for me.	*Yes*
Is there anything else I need to consider now?	*No*

You will rarely be surprised with the answers you get since they will make a lot of sense to you at the time. If at any stage the plumb-bob stops moving, or begins moving erratically, put it away and come back to it another time. Your deep mind is indicating that it is not ready to answer yet.

Your turn

Find something that will suffice as a plumb-bob. Establish a 'Yes' and a 'No' response, then you can ask it the question that led us to look at this interesting device, 'Is the left hemisphere of my brain dominant?' Repeat the question several times until you get a clear 'Yes' or 'No' signal.

Then double-check by asking, 'Is my right hemisphere dominant?', and you will soon notice a change to the opposite signal.

If you get a double 'Yes' or a double 'No' you are one of the small percentage of people who do not have a significant difference in the dominance rating of each hemisphere—both your hemispheres are about equal.

The right-brained student

Looking at the list of left-brain functions you will notice that traditional teaching is done mainly in this manner—logical, linear, detailed, analytical. This is fine for students who are left-brain-dominant or who have equal hemispheric dominance. However, for those who are right-brained—intuitive, creative, holistic, synthesizing—being at school sometimes seems like trying to swim upstream.

The methods in this book are helpful to all students whatever their brain dominance, but if your tendency is to use the right brain you will have a great bonus. *Superstudy* turns the stream around so that, perhaps for the first time in your life, you find yourself swimming with the current of scholastics instead of against it.

REVIEW

1 Discover which hemisphere dominates each part of your body.

2 Use a plumb-bob to contact your deep mind.

3 Use the plumb-bob to find out whether you are left- or right-brain-dominant.

7 The One-minute Turn-ons

There is nothing wrong with having both your hemispheres equally balanced in dominance. Most people have a preference for one side or the other, but again this is normal and natural, provided the differences are relatively small. If the differences are great, it could show that one hemisphere is coasting along with little or no exertion, while the other is working harder than necessary. If it were possible to stir the coasting side into action the dominant side would not have to take full responsibility for executing the function because the other side would also be helping. Can this be done? Can the coasting side be recruited to aid the dominant side?

Yes, it can. Here are some simple techniques that do make learning easier. They all involve simultaneous movement of both left and right parts of the body, sometimes known as cross-lateral motion. There is a paradigm that is used to explain the success of these movements. For over a century science has known that there is a direct connection between the hemispheres of the brain and opposite parts of the body. If a particular part of the left or the right hemisphere is electrically stimulated, then some part on the opposite side of the body will move. The paradigm takes this knowledge and reverses the model. By moving opposite parts of the body simultaneously the neuronal connections to the brain will activate both hemispheres simultaneously. It matters little which hemisphere is the normal controller of the function. When both sides of the body are moved together, then both hemispheres will be stimulated, and both can then be brought to work on the learning task.

Students doing these actions regularly liken the effects to finally learning how to move a wheelbarrow with two hands after having spent a lifetime trying to move it with one.

Marching

All over the world at the beginning of the school day, children are assembled in the quadrangle and then marched off into their classrooms, pacing out with their left foot as they swing their right hand forward, and then vice versa. Teachers will tell you that as soon as the children march into the room and sit down they are ready to begin work for the day. Not so a latecomer who misses out on the marching. It could take half an hour or more for the student to settle down. Ask marching girls, police, armed service people how they feel after routine marching, and they will talk about the energizing and centring effect. Have you ever paraded down the main street with your arms swinging in rhythm? It is a great feeling.

The essence of the march is the swinging forward of the arm as the opposite leg moves forward. Marching which keeps the arms locked into the sides is not recommended. The slow funeral march and the goose step do not have a beneficial effect, and neither does square-gaiting (swinging the left arm and foot together, and then the right arm and foot).

If marching around inside the house or out in the yard is not to your liking, similar benefit can be obtained by closing your study door and marching on the spot. It is good fun if you put on a tape of marching bands and really get into it. It helps if you imagine you are marching in a parade.

Walking

As with marching the free swing of the arms and opposite feet is the important movement. Benefit is reduced if the arm swing is impeded. If you are walking down to the local library, consider taking your backpack instead of a hand-held bag so you can have a beneficial walk there and back with your arms free of books.

Walking on the spot for a minute is an excellent pre-study activity.

Jogging

This is good, either on the spot in your room for a minute, or having a jog outdoors before your study session.

If it is the latter, jog up a steep or long slope where possible at some stage of your workout, so that your body encourages you to breathe more deeply than normal. Breathe strongly through your nose rather than your mouth. Have some tissues or a hanky handy! Natural deep breathing in exercise helps oxygenate the blood. It enriches the oxygen supply to the brain and produces a feeling of exhilaration and resourcefulness which improves your performance in a study period.

From the yogis it is known that inhaling and exhaling can be beneficially co-ordinated to the steps as you jog. To increase your energy levels you can inhale the breath on more steps than you exhale. For example, you can start counting jog steps and breathe deeply in to the count of five (1, 2, 3, 4, 5), and then exhale to the count of the next four steps (6, 7, 8, 9). Or breathe in for three steps, and breathe out for two, or in for six and out for five, and so on.

Notice that the sum of each set of in–out breaths is odd (4 in, 3 out = 7; 5 in, 4 out = 9; 3 in, 2 out = 5). This allows a change of the leading foot for each cycle:

Cycle 1: In-breath starts with the left foot.
Cycle 2: In-breath starts with the right foot.
Cycle 3: In-breath starts with the left foot again.

When you jog like this the pranic energy of the breath is spread equally over both sides of the body and the brain.

The significance of the odd number of the in–out breath cycle is that if breathing in is for a longer count than breathing out you will build up pranic energy, and this is the essence of vitality.

If you sometimes feel exhausted after a jog perhaps your in–out breath cycle is even (e.g. 4 in, 4 out) or perhaps it is energy depleting (e.g. 4 in, 6 out).

Sleep

The latter (fewer in-breaths than out-breaths) is a remedy for winding down your spinning head after a busy late-night study session. In bed, as you are ready to drift off to dreamland, take your heartbeat as the metronome and breathe out more than you breathe in (e.g. out 5, in 4). You will soon sink into calmness and slumber.

Mini-trampolines

Mini-trampolines are a useful asset, especially in winter if you do not like running in the sub-zero temperatures of frosty mornings. Any of the above exercises can be done on the mini-tramp. There are plenty of variations of the leg and foot movements that can be enhanced on the mini-tramp.

While bouncing, experiment with these cycles:
- right hand touches raised left knee, and vice versa;
- right hand to left heel in front of body, and vice versa;
- right hand to left heel behind body, and vice versa;
- scissor, with arms and legs straight;
- left leg straight out in front, right hand touches it, and vice versa.

Anything that simultaneously moves the right leg with the left arm or the left leg with the right arm is suitable. These exercises can also be done on the floor or the jogging track. The advantage of the mini-tramp is that it is much kinder to the feet and the spine.

Eyeballing the brain

If for some reason you are unable to do the whole body exercises above, your eyes alone can be used to activate both hemispheres. Do these two exercises as you read through them:

1 Union Jack

In a sitting or standing position look straight ahead, and keep your nose perfectly still in space. This is the 'centre' position.

Keeping your nose still, find a distant point straight ahead, up high in your visual field, that you can focus both eyes on. Then centre.

Keeping your nose still, focus on a distant point as low as possible. Then centre.

Keeping your nose still, find a distant horizontal point as far to the left as you can focus both eyes on. Then centre.

Repeat to the right. Then centre.

Now focus on a point up to the high left (north-west). Centre.

Down to the low right (south-east). Centre.

Up to the high right (north-east). Centre.

Finally, down to the low left (south-west). Centre.

By the end your eyes have traversed the bars of the British flag, the Union Jack.

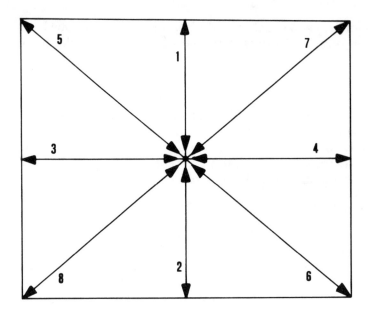

2   Elton John

Pretend you are sitting facing Elton John only 10 centimetres away. He is wearing a pair of enormous round sunglasses, the kind he is famous for.

Look at the bridge of his nose, and without moving your head use your eyes to follow one of his lenses up and around in a clockwise direction, until your eyes come back to the bridge of his nose. Continue moving your eyes, this time in a counter-clockwise motion around his other imaginary lens and back to the bridge of his nose.

Repeat the cycle several times.

You may feel dizzy the first few times. This is a good sign, for it shows that some circuits that have not been used for a while are now being exercised.

The exercise can also easily be done with your eyes closed—so you can secretly do it in the middle of a class!

Nostrilling

Even the nostrils can be used for a quick turn-on, though it is a good idea to have tissues or a hanky handy for this.

Press one nostril closed, and breathe strongly and very deeply, in and out ten times through the other.

Repeat with the other nostril.

You will notice an immediate improvement in the clarity of your thought with this technique.

Brain massages

Two bilateral areas where massage can be used are on the ears and on the forehead.

1 Bother bumps

To find the forehead points, look straight ahead into the bathroom mirror. Directly up from the pupils of your eyes, a couple of centimetres above your eyebrows, you will find two gentle bumps on the forehead, one over the left eye and one over the right.

Gently rub these, with one index finger on either bump. Alternatively, use one hand with the thumb on one bump and all the other fingerpads on the other bump.

This will stimulate both hemispheres, and increase your clarity of thought, especially if you have been under stress. You will see people using this massage unconsciously when something is bothering them.

2 Eary sensations

Rub around the skull directly behind both ears, and inside the outer shell on the circumference of each ear. This is helpful when you are concentrating on listening to long speeches or lectures. Do not be concerned about being precise. Just give a good rub with your fingers and thumbs to both ears and the part of the skull they would cover if you pressed them hard against the skull.

Listening to speech is primarily a left-brain function, but with this massage you can trick both hemispheres into working on the task. Your concentration is much better after this quick treatment.

REVIEW

Before every study session, spend a minute on some of these:
marching
walking
jogging
the Union Jack (eyes)
the Elton John (eyes)
nostrilling (nose)
bother bumps (forehead massage)
eary sensations (ear massage)

8   Fine-tuning the Yin and the Yang

Australians think of Western medical science as being traditional, and of Chinese medical science as being 'alternative'. In East Asia the perspective is reversed. Chinese medicine has a tradition thousands of years old; Western drug- and scalpel-based medicine is young by comparison. Traditional Chinese medicine is by no means primitive. Just like Western medicine, it is constantly being advanced, despite its long history. In Asian cities today Western and traditional Chinese hospitals can be found side by side, both equally respected by the patients. We would have fewer ills if the same respect existed in Australia.

Traditional Chinese medicine maps out life energies in the body. The energies flow in two directions, the Yin and the Yang. They flow through the body in meridians, and they also carry information to and from the brain. The functioning of the brain can be enhanced by manipulating the meridians using acupressure and massage.

It is easy to find these acupoints in your own body. Find them as you read about each one, follow the instructions, and notice the effect they have on you.

Acupoints

1   The shenque acupoint

This is right on your belly button. There is no need to strip. The massage is fully effective through your clothing.

Press a finger of one hand on the navel, and jiggle your navel. Simultaneously use a finger and thumb of your other hand to rub two points which are the slight depressions just below the bumps at the inside ends of your collarbones.

Do this for a few seconds, then change hands and massage gently for a few more seconds.

This is helpful for reading comprehension.

2   The fengchi

Again, gently massage your navel with a finger of one hand.

Simultaneously use your other hand to massage the fengchi acupoints. These are in the slight hollows at the base of your skull between the ears and the back of the neck.

After a few seconds reverse your hands.

Use this for any type of problem solving.

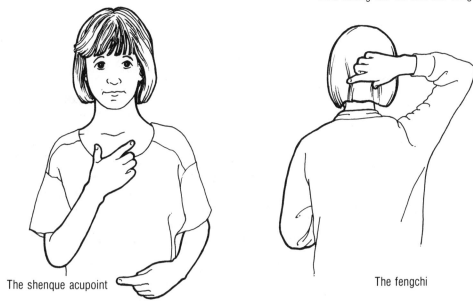

The shenque acupoint

The fengchi

3 The renzhong

This point is on your face, directly between the bottom of your nose and the centre of your upper lip. Press this point with a finger and jiggle it.

With a finger from your other hand, rub the base of your spine (the end of the coccyx).

Gently massage for a few moments, then swap hand positions.

This is good preparation for writing an assignment, or giving a talk to a tutorial or seminar group. It looks weird if people do not understand what you are doing, so go to a toilet cubicle or other private area to do this before the class starts.

The renzhong

4 The brain meridian

The meridian affecting the brain runs up the middle of the front of your body from a point about 15 centimetres below your navel, straight up to your bottom lip.

Run the fingertips of one hand several times up this meridian, starting below your navel, moving up over the stomach, up the chest and throat, to your bottom lip. Then take your hand straight out in front of your mouth to arms-length in a big circle down to the starting point again. It is easier to do this if you are standing up.

If you are feeling 'spaced out' for any reason, do this in the opposite direction—from your bottom lip down to the bottom of your belly area, since you may need to encourage energy flow in the opposite direction.

Use this to prepare for holistic activities, such as getting an overview of a new topic or pre-scanning the work you want to finish in a study period.

5 The thymus

This gland is situated a few centimetres down from the top of the vertical central breastbone. It is the regulator of the life-force known to the Chinese as 'Ch'i', which circulates round the body and is the source of vitality.

If you are feeling generally depleted of energy, thump your central chest bone near its top a dozen times. Use your open hand with the four fingers in line together. Thump hard enough with your fingertips to get a hollow knocking sound.

You can do this whenever you think of it; it cannot be overdone. Make it a regular part of your pre-study routine.

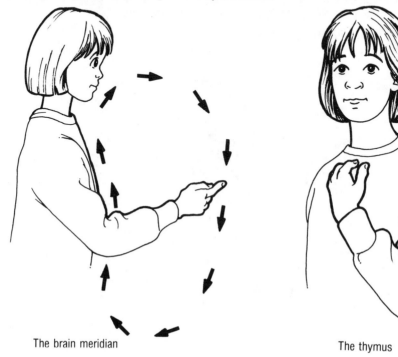

The brain meridian   The thymus

These simple exercises are potent, and the beneficial effect is cumulative. Use each one daily for at least a week before deciding whether to incorporate it regularly into your pre-study preparation.

Professional therapists who use techniques such as these are called kinesiologists. Kinesiology is a growing discipline in Australia. Disabilities in learning can frequently be quickly remedied by an educational kinesiologist.

Some state education departments in Australia already have teachers in their schools who are trained in kinesiology. A question is directed to the student, and the kinesiologist then tests the strength of a selected muscle of the student. A muscle which remains strong in response to the question is indicating a 'Yes' answer and a muscle which weakens indicates a 'No'. The change in muscle strength has nothing to do with whether the student wants to answer 'Yes' or 'No'. It is a deep-mind response, similar to the 'Yes' and 'No' responses you can get on your own with a plumb-bob. Working with the 'Yes' or 'No' answers the kinesiologist can rapidly diagnose malfunctions in the student's energy flow which are affecting the hemispheric balance of the brain. The kinesiologist will then prescribe activities such as the cross-lateral exercises listed in the previous chapter, or exercises like some of the ones in this chapter which work on the Yin and Yang energy flows within the body.

Water

Many people need to drink a glass of tap water before they start to study. Through muscle testing countless clients over the years, kinesiologists have discovered unusual properties of the glass of common tap water. Just like a car battery, it is critical that the water level of the body be topped up for optimal brain work.

One way of explaining this is that the brain needs sufficient water to act as an electrolyte for its electrical processes to operate smoothly. This is only a metaphorical expression, however, as the exact reason for the effect of the water is not completely understood. Nevertheless, drinking a glass of water before studying is beneficial for most people. It is an excellent precaution, even if you do not know whether you need it or not. An extra glass can do no harm.

Muscle testing shows that the drink must be straight water. The body is unable to extract the water in the form it needs from any other hot or cold beverages such as tea, coffee, soft drinks, milk, or fruit juices. To be useful it needs to be clear water from the tap, or, even better, filtered rainwater or springwater that is not tainted by fluoride or chlorine.

Tension easers

Newborn babies have not learned to put sufficient tension into their shoulder or neck muscles to keep their heads erect. Parents take care to support their babies' heads for the first few months or else the head will literally flop about on the top of the spine. Babies soon learn to hold their heads up by tensing their shoulders and necks. As the infants develop into maturity they need to keep their heads erect for almost every moment of their waking life. Since it is always necessary to keep some tension there in the neck it is a convenient place for adults to store the extra stress of everyday living that cannot be dissipated during the day. The excess tightness results in chronic tension of the area, and restricts the flow of energy to and from the body and the brain.

There are simple exercises which will work to get rid of the tension and improve the flow of energy. The exercises will help to loosen the muscles of the shoulder and the neck so that the brain can receive a full and steady unrestricted blood and oxygen supply.

Do the exercises as you read through them.

1   Circular shrug

Shrug your shoulders up as close as possible to your ears.

Then continue the shoulder shrug in an arc to your front, so that your shoulders hunch forward.

Continue the arc downwards, pushing your shoulders as far as possible away from your ears.

Continue arcing around, as far back as possible without craning your neck forward.

Complete the circle by rolling your shoulders up to your ears again.

Do several more rotating shrugs in the same circular direction.

Reverse the direction, and do several more of the circular shrugs.

Circular shrug

2   Cross-your-heart massage

With your right hand, reach up past your throat to the long muscle across the very top of your left shoulder. Massage it quite strongly as you consciously begin to relax it.

Repeat with the left hand, reaching across to the right shoulder.

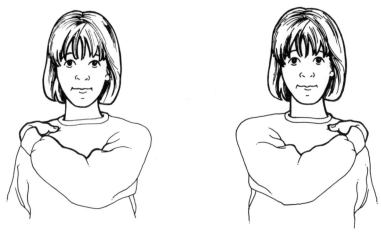

Cross-your heart massage

3   The swan

Stand or sit up tall, and look straight ahead.

Very slowly sweep your eyes horizontally over your right shoulder as far you can comfortably turn your head, as if you are trying to see something directly behind you without moving your shoulders.

Centre, and repeat slowly over the left shoulder. Centre.

Repeat the cycle several times.

You may hear some gravelly crunches as you are turning. This is a good sign. The motion is freeing up parts of the neck that need to be moved more often. If the noise is so loud or the movement so jerky that it worries you, ease your mind by having a chat to your doctor or chiropractor next time you see one of them.

The swan

4 The head cock

Look straight ahead, and try to touch your left ear slowly to your left shoulder without raising your shoulder. Centre.

Likewise, try to touch your right ear to your right shoulder.

Repeat the cycle.

The head cock

Stomach salves

Some people carry more tension in the stomach than in the neck and shoulder region. If you are one of these, here are two remedies to ease the discomfort. Do them as you read them.

1 Sitting bones

Sit on a kitchen chair or other firm-seated study chair. Imagine there is a skyhook attached to the top of your head at the centre. This hook connects to an elastic strip that is stretched up to a point directly above you in the ceiling. Pretend it is lightly pulling you upwards, and in so doing your spine becomes straightened and you no longer stoop over the desk.

As you begin to straighten all the way from your head to your bottom you will begin to notice that you are sitting on two bones. Rock your pelvis forward and back a little until you can clearly feel the two sitting bones. The anatomical term for these bones is the ischial tuberosity, and they are the bottom of the pelvis.

When you can feel these bones, you are in the correct posture for long hours of comfortable study. Sitting in this position will alleviate not only stomach tension but also excess tension from your whole body. When your study session ends you will still be fresh and clear in your body and mind.

2 Belly breathing

If you fill a rubberized hot-water bottle from the kettle the water goes straight down to the bottom of the bottle first, and causes it to bulge at the base. The bulge becomes bigger as more water enters and spreads upwards to the middle. Finally, when the bottle can stretch no more, the water reaches the neck. This is a model for belly breathing.

Sit on your sitting bones, or stand.

Imagine your lungs are like two hot-water bottles. Exhale completely. Pretend the air you start breathing is like the water flowing in. It will help if you push your stomach out a little at the start.

Feel the air flowing right down to the bottom of your lungs, causing them to expand. As the air slowly comes in, it fills the lungs from the bottom to the middle and from the middle to the top. Gently fill them as full as you can.

When they are topped right up, let the breath surge out in a series of short bursts as if you were silently coughing, or saying, 'Ha, ha, ha, ha, ha, ha, haaaaaa', finally emptying your lungs of the last traces of breath.

Do several of these at any stage of your study session to get an extra burst of energy.

REVIEW

Before every study session drink a glass of water, and spend a minute on several of the following.

Acupoints
The shenque—reading comprehension
The fengchi—problem-solving
The renzhong—writing, doing exams, giving talks
Brain meridian—previewing and reviewing big topics
The thymus—general.

Tension easers
Circular shrug—shoulders
Cross-your-heart massage—shoulders
The swan—neck
The head cock—neck
Sitting bones—stomach
Belly breathing—stomach.

9 Mind-clearing

You have noticed that one of the first things teachers do when they come into a classroom is to check the whiteboard or blackboard. If it has writing on it they wipe it off. It would be pointless to start to teach new material when the board is filled with information that is not relevant to the current session.

Do you often feel that your mind is like a blackboard filled up with all sorts of stuff that has nothing to do with what you are about to study? What if you could clear your mind before you start to study as easily and thoroughly as the teachers clean the board?

You can. There are two ways to do it.

1   The first one is so simple you will wonder why you have not thought of it as a study technique before. To clear your mind just jot down on a piece of paper or in your diary whatever is buzzing around in there. Do you have to remember to pay the electricity bill or to buy more bread? Jot it down, and then put the diary away, or put the paper safely in your pocket to be taken out and acted upon at the appropriate time.

2   The second way is mind-clearing with relaxation and multi-sensory imagery.

The two-minute relaxation

There are hundreds of ways to achieve general physical relaxation. A television set is very effective. So is gentle music, yoga, a couple of beers, meditation, self-hypnosis, a warm bath, concentrating on your breath, sunbathing, laughing gas, and plenty of other ways.

Relaxation is well worth the time it takes because of the clarity of mind you will have after doing it. I refer to the drug-free type of relaxation here, because drugs and alcohol produce confusion rather than clarity. If you are not already involved in a daily relaxation routine you are missing out on a free, pleasant and inexhaustible supply of life energy. If it is new to you, the quickest way to learn how to do it is to use an audio cassette. You can get a commercial relaxation tape from the local library or you could buy one in the local shopping centre, but these are usually much longer than you need.

Making your own is easy and fun, so get whatever you need ready, and have a go now. A couple of minutes is how long the tape should run, so a C60 cassette is fine. When you are recording do it in time with your natural deep breathing.

If you have another cassette player play some gentle instrumental music on it while you are making the recording, so that your voice comes out with a musical backing. The peaceful music in the background has two purposes. First, it helps in the relaxation process. Second, the music activates the right hemisphere. Talking is mainly processed by the left hemisphere, so when it is accompanied by music both sides of the brain are turned on together, bringing the whole brain into action for your study.

When you are ready, read the following onto the cassette. Pause for a few seconds where indicated.

Put your feet flat on the floor.

Push your bottom against the back of the chair.

Close your eyes, and take a few deep breaths.

Take a very deep breath in. (*Pause*)

Breathe out, and imagine that all the muscles in your face are relaxing—scalp, eyes, nose, lips, tongue, cheek, jaw—just pretend they are relaxing.

Take another deep breath in. (*Pause*)

This time, as you breathe out, imagine you are letting go your throat and neck muscles, your shoulders, upper arms, lower arms, hands and fingers. Just let them go, let them relax, and as you do so, become aware of the chair you are sitting in holding you safely, firmly and securely, allowing you to relax even more.

Breathe in again deeply. (*Pause*)

As you breathe out, pretend you are letting go of the big muscles in your chest and stomach, your upper back, and your lower back and your bottom, all those big muscles in your trunk, just let them go, let them relax.

Breathe in again. (*Pause*)

Breathe out, and imagine you are letting go of the muscles in your thighs, legs, feet and toes.

Take another deep breath in. (*Pause*)

Just check through your body to see if there are any tight places, and if there are, just notice them as you breathe out.

Now you can already feel that you are more relaxed than you were just a few moments ago, so just continue to breathe in and out deeply and gently (add 'as you listen to the music' if you have gentle music playing).

Each time you breathe in, imagine the oxygen coming into your brain to improve your concentration and memory; each time you breathe out just let yourself relax a little more.

As your body and mind move easily into this relaxed state for optimum learning you can say to yourself the word 'Superstudy' several times (*pause*), and know that just repeating this word at any time you wish in the future makes it easier and easier for you to return to the relaxed state you are now in.

Notes:

1 You may prefer to put the relaxation into 'I' language—'I put my feet flat on the floor. I push my bottom against the back of the chair . . .', and so on. That works equally well.

2 Your bottom is pushed against the back of the chair so that your spine is kept straight without effort. If you like to lie down to do the relaxation, omit the second instruction.

3 Imagination is the key. It is not necessary to really relax or to get into a zombie-like state. Just imagine you are relaxed, and even if it does not happen the first few times keep doing it once or twice a day for a week or so, and soon you will discover that you are relaxing without noticing it. The state you want is just the same as if you were watching your favourite show on television. It is easy to reach.

4 After you have made the recording, sit down and follow your own instructions.

Instant relaxation

The oftener you do this two-minute relaxation the better you will get. In a month or two you will be able to dispense with the anatomical progression, and achieve adequate relaxation in a few seconds even without a cassette.

You will be able to do this just by taking a few deep breaths and scanning your body to become aware of any tension. If you find any tightness in your body just be aware of it, and this in itself will lead to the tension lessening. Or you can dissolve the tension. Imagine your breath is a healing warm gas, take the breath in through your mouth, and then pretend to direct it to the tension, no matter where the tense part is in your body.

The slightly relaxed state you achieve with the two-minute relaxation is more than just a mind-clearing technique. It is the optimal state you should achieve for listening, reading, writing, examinations, in short for everything relating to your study. Here is the reason.

The rules of our community force us to repress a lot of our energies. When drivers see parking inspectors writing out a ticket for their cars they may have a fleeting urge to hit the inspectors, or at least to yell a little at the inspectors. But drivers know the long-term consequences of this would not be in their best interests! So they bottle up the anger, and eventually it goes away. But where does it go? It is converted to tension and stored in their musculature, where it impedes the flow of life-energy. And there it stays forever, unless they express their anger or do some hard physical exercise or regularly relax their entire body. Other emotions, such as grief, hurt, and fear, are also regularly repressed, and held as tension. Laughter and crying are antidotes to this cumulative process, but you would need to laugh or cry for an hour a day to break even. The most practical solution is relaxation.

Regular relaxation eases the physical tension in the musculature, and thus releases the life-force from its work of holding the muscles more tightly than necessary. The life-force can then be channelled into the work of concentrating, using the exercises of the previous two chapters.

The longer you continue to relax, the stronger the benefits; do it for up to about 20 minutes, twice a day. The 40 minutes taken up by relaxation is more than rewarded by the increased clarity of thought right through the day, and even, when necessary, late into the night. In Chapter 11 you will discover how the time you are spending in relaxation can be used to effortlessly rote-learn your study material.

Students do it anywhere

It is useful to learn to relax in different body positions. The most practical are in a chair or on the floor.

1 In a chair

The ability to relax while in a seated position will allow you to choose from a number of alternatives. As well as in your study chair at home, you can relax in a seated position in the library, a lecture hall, in a car, in a church pew, and so on. The last two are useful.

(a) *The car*

If you have your own car, it will mostly be parked near to where you will be studying. After you park, move over to the passenger's seat to relax. Then other drivers will know you are not about to drive off, so they will not wait for you to leave the parking space. If you are relaxing at home, make sure your family and friends know that when you are in the car you are not to be disturbed.

(b) *The church*

A church pew is an excellent place to relax if there is no service in progress at the time. Even an atheist will find the quiet atmosphere conducive to relaxation. Anyone else there will think you are praying, so you will not be disturbed during your relaxation, however long you stay.

2   On the floor

This one can be done in the privacy of your room, or on the grass under a shady tree on a hot afternoon, and it is worth learning. It is called the Alexander horizontal position, and comes originally from the physical discipline known as the Alexander Technique.

To do this, lie flat on your back on the floor (or the grass), with your head resting on two audio cassette cases stacked one on top of the other (or some other object of a similar size) so that your head is raised several centimetres from the floor. Now draw your knees up until your feet are flat on the floor, a little further apart than the width of your shoulders. Let your knees flop so they lean slightly inwards. Your arms can fall symmetrically wherever they are comfortable. Why not go through the two-minute relaxation now in this position for a comparison between the seated and horizontal positions?

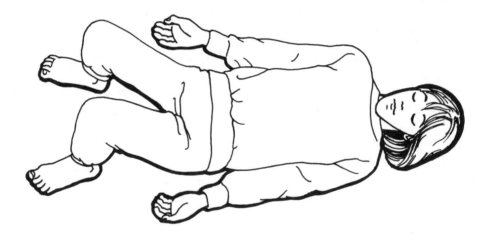

The advantage of this position is that it automatically arranges your spine (and therefore your head and trunk) into the best natural posture. It has a training effect on your body, such that if you hold your spine in the same way when you are standing up you will be in your anatomically best position. Because you are no longer unconsciously using your muscles to force your body into inefficient posture you will use least of your life-energy this way when you are sitting, standing or walking. The energy will be released and be available for the various areas of your learning. You may discover, as many people have, that the correcting effect is as though you were running around all your life with your brakes on, and through the Alexander position you find out how to release them.

Applied relaxation

After a week or so of practising the two-minute physical relaxation you can start to use it in various ways.

1 Experiencing life-energy

After you play your home-made two-minute relaxation tapescript through once, let it continue to play on through the blank part (it is up to you whether you have the other cassette playing gentle music in the background). When the blank part arrives simply recall the script and follow it through in your mind several times more. You will find that the more you recall and repeat the two-minute relaxation from your head to your toes the better your overall relaxation for that session will be. You will start to become aware of the sensations in your entire body. Perhaps you will experience a tingling in some areas, which indicates your life-energy is beginning to flow again in those areas. It is a major gain for you when this happens.

2 Dealing with pain

Pain can distract you from your study. If you notice tension or pain in any part of your body, spend a few moments acknowledging it. Pain is the way the nervous system tells you that it needs more life-energy. The easiest way to direct energy there is to imagine you are bathing it in a sphere of white light. No matter if the discomfort is on the inside or the surface of your body, pretend you are sending white light to heal it. You will be surprised how the area becomes more comfortable by just acknowledging it and applying the white light. If the pain does not respond, you should see a doctor.

REVIEW

---

1 After your glass of water, and your one-minute turn-ons, jot down anything that is on your mind. Then play your home-made cassette for a few minutes to relax and to remove the mental clutter in preparation for study.

2 Learn both the seated and horizontal relaxation positions so that you are able to relax quietly and easily almost anywhere.

3 Use applied relaxation to experience raw life-energy and to obviate pain that interferes with your concentration.

---

10   Multi-sensory Imagery

The sandpit memory

Imagine you are holding a bucket of water over a child's sandpit. The bucket has a single small hole in it, such that the water trickles out onto the sand. When it hits the sand it forms a tiny hole, and disappears through the surface.

Now imagine the same bucket of water with a dozen similar holes in its base. This time the water comes out in a dozen trickles like a shower. It pours over the sand so quickly it cannot be absorbed. Within seconds it wets the sand, and begins to run off. Trickles from different holes in the bucket join together to form rivulets which gouge miniature valleys in the sand-hills. Rapidly the whole topography of the sandpit is changed into tiny cliffs and lakes, rivers and deltas.

The sandpit is the memory system of the mind. Traditional learning is the bucket with a single hole. Learn something once this way and you are lucky if it makes an impression at all. Multi-sensory learning is the bucket with lots of holes. Use lots of trickles of water in your learning, and you will make such a strong impression on your sandpit memory that you can recall it instantly years into the future.

The trickles of water are your senses. Your five primary senses are seeing, hearing, touching, tasting and smelling. You also have buckets of other senses—temperature, pressure, emotion, colour, balance, pain, and so on. When you develop these and use them deliberately in your studies, your understanding will be easier and your memory more profound. You can develop these rapidly by using techniques from suggestopedia, neuro-linguistic programming and psychosynthesis, which have been blended and strengthened in the sections which follow.

Remembering the fun

After you have made the basic two-minute relaxation tape, you can make different additions to it. Each of these will give you practice in developing your skill in creating multi-sensory images. The images have a special effect on memory retention, which you can read about in the next chapter on Concerts.

With the first of these you will be able to recapture the natural joy of learning we all have when we are very young. Learning in its natural state must be a pleasant experience because it is an evolutionary necessity. If it were unpleasant, humans would have no incentive ever to learn anything, and we could not have evolved to our dominant place in the world—people would still be fending off wild animals with sticks and stones. When we were young we learned with joy to make noises, and to sit up and talk and walk and feed ourselves, to hold things, and later to ride a bike, or to write our names, or to make a piece of toast, and so on. We can now harness this natural joy of learning, and use it.

When you make this additional part of the tape you can recall a real incident from your childhood or think of an imaginary one. Both work equally well. Here is what to say at the end of the physical relaxation part of the cassette. It is in the first person ('I' language) to illustrate a different style for you; but continue to use the second person 'you' language of the two-minute relaxation if you prefer.

And now I am going way, way back in time, back to when I was very young, back to when I was learning something for the very first time, full of the natural wonder and joy that comes whenever I learn something new, and in my memory or my imagination I can see the scene once more. What do I see around me? *(Pause about five seconds at each asterisk)*

Do I see myself as though I am in a movie, or am I in my body looking out through my own eyes? *

Am I alone, or are there other people with me? *

If there are other people, who are they? *

What colours are their clothes, and what other colours can I see around me? *

What clothing am I wearing? *

How does the clothing feel against my skin? *

Is it daytime or night-time? *

Am I warm or cool? *

Am I sitting or standing? Am I still or moving? *

What am I doing with my body? *

What scents or aromas can I smell? *

What is the taste in my mouth? *

While I am learning this wonderful and exciting new thing how does my head feel? *

How does my stomach feel? *

Now I touch my index finger lightly to my thumb, and I gradually press them harder together. As I do so, I turn up the intensity of the joy I experience while I am learning this wonderfully fascinating new thing. Pressing harder and harder together, and becoming more and more joyful. Then I relax, and let my finger and thumb rest. *

> Now once again I press finger and thumb together as I increase the intensity of that joyful experience. Harder and harder, and more and more fun!. Now I relax my finger and thumb again. *
>
> Now I know I have a sign I can use whenever I want to re-experience that pleasant feeling again in any current learning situation. *
>
> I now have a choice. The choice is in experiencing any type of learning situation as pleasant or otherwise. If I choose it to be pleasant I can make the sign with my finger and thumb, and all the joy of early learning comes back to me. *
>
> In a few moments I will begin my study time, and I will continue with my study in this relaxed state. *
>
> Now I open my eyes, wriggle my fingers and toes, and take a deep breath before I stretch and begin my work. *

As soon as you have finished recording this, take a few minutes out to sit down and enjoy it. It is something that you can repeat from time to time, and each time you may get different images. In remembering the fun of natural learning in childhood, students are sometimes moved to tears of joy when they realize that these wonderful times have not vanished forever, and are available for accessing whenever they are sought.

This particular visualization has the excellent feature of providing a trigger. Whenever you find yourself in a tense or nasty situation from now on, press your finger and thumb together and you can trigger a flood of resourcefulness back into your body to bolster your ability to deal with whatever the ugly situation is.

Sometimes students will say that they cannot 'see' anything when they imagine. This is fine. All they need to do is to follow what the tape is saying, and to remember or imagine things whenever the tape suggests them. It is not necessary for them to actually 'see' anything.

Open imagery

It is a good idea to have several multi-sensory image-building scripts available. Listening to the same one time and again can get boring for some people.

In the 'remembering the fun' script there is plenty of room for you to develop various sensory images which can change each time you play it through. This is done by using questions: 'What do I see around me? Am I alone or are there other people with me? . . .' This is called open imagery. Every replay can give you a completely different experience.

At other times it is helpful to be able to produce precise and vivid imagery, especially in the concert session (see the next chapter). Next is an example of the kind of scripts you can tailor to suit your own specific needs and preferences. You will notice that there are no questions in this one. The statements are all direct.

Directed imagery

Imagine you are having a weekend holiday in a lavish five star-hotel in Hawaii. You are lounging on a deck-chair in the gardens not far from the swimming pool. Imagine the texture of the deck-chair pressing against you as it firmly supports your body. *(*Pause about five seconds*)

It is a very warm afternoon and you are under the shade of the gently swaying palm trees. Imagine the warmth seeping into your body. *

Sometimes a playful breeze wafts over you, bringing coolness for a few moments. *

The breeze brings tantalizing aromas from the outdoor bistro; the smell of fresh baked bread mixes with the smell of your favourite dishes. *

You motion to a waiter, who is at your side almost instantly, and you ask for a plate of tropical fruit for starters. He walks briskly off. *

While he is getting the fruit you notice that a small group of musicians has started playing music on steel guitars and a vibraphone—music that is typically Hawaiian. Listen to the music as you rest in relaxation and tranquillity. *

The waiter has returned already with the plate of exotic fruits. Just look at the deep rich colours of the pineapple, * the pawpaw, * the water-melon, * the mango. *

Take a toothpick, and lift a piece of pawpaw to your mouth. It tastes so much nicer than the pawpaw at home. This one is so creamy and full-bodied. *

Look around you and take in the luxurious surroundings of this first-class resort—the sparkling water in the swimming pool, * the meticulously tended shrubs and flowers, * the manicured lawns, * the beautiful sculptures dotted here and there. *

Let the feeling of pleasure permeate your whole being for a few moments more *

And when you are ready, slowly become aware that you are back in the present moment. Wriggle your fingers and toes, stretch and take a deep breath or two. *

You can make up any number of these yourself—perhaps at the beach, in a park, on a bushwalk, on a boat, in a hot air balloon, and so on. Your imagination is limitless.

Here is another that is useful if you are studying in a place where there are a lot of distractions. This one has a combination of open imagery and directed imagery.

Your crystal study

You are standing on the sandy shores of a beautiful lake on a fine warm day. Feel the sun warming your face and hands. *(*Pause about five seconds*)

Near you is a long sturdy wooden bridge leading to a small island. As you step onto the bridge you notice that the section you are walking on is painted red. *

You continue along the bridge and the red paint fades into the colour orange. *

Listen to the seagulls crying as they wheel overhead.

Walking further along, and the colour once again changes, this time to yellow. *

Take a deep breath, and smell the freshness of the water you are walking over. *

The yellow section in turn changes into a bright shade of green. *

And the green merges into a deep blue. *

As you near the end of the bridge the blue becomes purple. *

Stepping off the bridge onto the island you see a little track leading off into the bushes. Follow this track, and you come to a clearing. This is where you are to create your own study retreat—a place that you alone can go to whenever you need to work in solitude, away from the distractions of the world around you.

The first thing to do is to make the structure itself. *

You can make it with any material you like. Crystal? Mud brick? Anything! Your imagination is so powerful you can make it in a moment. Make it now. *

Put a door into the structure so that you can enter. Make the lock on the door of a special type that responds only to the touch of your own fingerprint. That way only you can ever go inside. It is your own sanctuary. *

Now walk up to the door, and put your finger on it. As it opens you can look inside. There is nothing but space in here. How would you like to furnish it for your ultimate comfort and concentration? What about the walls and the floor? How would you like them to be? *

Remember to have plenty of natural ventilation and light. *

Choose a fine desk for yourself and put it in the centre of the room. *

A firm sturdy chair is the kind that will keep you comfortably seated for hours. Custom-make one for yourself now, using the finest of materials. *

Level with the top of your desk and right behind it, you can have your large television screen or monitor. Its remote control panel is next to your hand when you are sitting at the desk. This will be helpful to you in many ways. *

Do you need lamps or pens or paper supplies? Fresh flowers? Anything at all that you would like, add it to your study now. *

Your study is now comfortably appointed, and you know how easy it is to change or add or take out anything at any time. *

Now it is time to leave, so just come over to the door. See how it opens automatically from the inside when you want to leave. Step outside into the glorious sunshine once again. *

Look back, watch the door close and lock, and admire the excellent structure you have created. *

Now follow the path back to the bridge. *

Step onto the purple start of the bridge. *

Walk back along the blue section, * the green, * the yellow, * the orange. *

As you come to the red section, step off the bridge onto the sandy shore of the beautiful lake again, and when you are ready you will find yourself here in the present time. Wriggle your fingers and toes, stretch, and take a deep breath or two. *

Whenever you are studying to a deadline and there are distractions around you, let the distractions continue if you cannot stop them or avoid them. Simply enter your crystal study. You will be able to work better in here, whatever is happening around you.

Telecasting your own triumphs

The television screen you installed in the crystal study is of great value to you. It shows you how you look when you are being successful and resourceful. On it you can rehearse any situation in which you will need courage and centredness. A job interview, a speech, a confrontation, a court appearance, an examination, or whatever. All you do is to imagine how the situation would run if everything turned out the best possible way.

Imagine yourself being relaxed and confident. See yourself sitting, standing or moving with easy graceful balance. Hear yourself speaking in that particular voice quality and tone which reminds you that you are resourceful and confident. As you look at this wonderful person who is yourself, you know this person has the poise and ability to deal effectively with any situation. Imagine all the threatening things transforming into factors that help and support you. Use as many multi-sensory images as you can muster. Run it through on the television screen several times until you get used to the feeling of success.

As an example of how you can use your crystal study television screen, here is a way you can get rid of examination phobia.

Dissolving exam anxiety

Go across the bridge to your crystal study and sit down.

With the remote control, turn on the television screen, and select a channel that has you on it one month after the examination. *(Pause about five seconds)*

Watch the screen and see how pleased you look when you think back to the exam last month, and how happy you were with the results. Step inside your screen image, and feel your happy feelings, see the successful result sheet, smell, hear, touch and taste things that may be around you. *

Roll back the days until you come to the time immediately after the exam has finished. Let yourself feel the relief of having performed to your best during the examination, and notice how confident you are now that you are assured of passing the exam. *

Go back to the last few minutes of the exam. You are scanning through the pages of answers just to check all is well. You are feeling excited and jubilant because you have planned the timing of the answers so well that you have these moments available at the end for checking. You have completed all the questions that you needed to—some better than others to be sure, but nevertheless all are adequately answered. Your breathing is deep and relaxed whenever you notice it. *

Go back to the beginning of the exam now. Look how self-assured you are, reading carefully through the paper so that you know exactly what the examiners require, planning how much time to give each question and which order to answer them in. Perhaps you are jotting down key words next to each question to jog your memory when you come to answer them later in the exam. Your breathing is deep and relaxed. Perhaps you are using the thumb-and-index-finger trigger to maintain your calmness and sense of fun. The questions you need to answer seem familiar to you, and you know you have enough information to answer them. *

Now wind back to just before you are called into the examination. Look around you and see the nervous faces of the other students. Listen to their negative babbling. What a shame they have not had the common sense to prepare themselves the way you have! You have done your one-minute turn-ons at a convenient time and place today. You feel just a little apprehensive, but that is healthy. It will help your performance as soon as you walk into the examination room. You are using your trigger to reduce excess tension, and you are monitoring your deep and gentle breathing. Smell the fresh air around you. Each time you breathe in imagine the oxygen coming into your brain to help you remember and think well during the exam. Each time you breathe out just relax a little more. *

Back now to the night before the exam. Your preparation is complete, and it is bed-time. You have done your best to be ready for this exam, and that is all you need. Tomorrow you will do the best you can, and that is all anyone can ask of themselves. You have checked the equipment you need to take with you, and all is in order. When you sleep tonight it may be deep sleep or it may be light sleep. Whatever you get will be exactly the right amount of sleep that you need to perform at your peak tomorrow. You feel quietly confident of your performance tomorrow. *

Now, come right back to a few months before the exam. Already your preparation has started. You have planned your study timetable for this unit. You may be using papers from previous exams to regularly practise answering questions under simulated exam conditions. You are determined to pass no matter what. You feel great for having made this commitment to yourself. You are willing and able to deal with any barrier that may try to come between you and your target of succeeding in this exam. To end, in no more than five seconds rapidly replay the whole sequence from now to a month after the exam, and end with your happy feelings of accomplishment. *

Emergency remedy

Here is a 'twenty-second Band-Aid' to use if you suddenly find yourself in a nasty situation that you have not had time to prevent by doing the above anxiety-eliminating exercise.

1   Go to your crystal study centre, and turn on the TV.

2   As you take in a very deep breath, see yourself on the screen exactly as you are now in the nasty situation. Breathe out.

3   Take another deep breath, and superimpose a miniscule image of yourself being poised and confident. Put this tiny image in the middle of the

image of you that is already on the TV screen. Exhale strongly as you expand the new image, so that when you have finished exhaling this image entirely blots out the old image. Jump inside the image of the new you.

4 Repeat step 2 several more times, making your new images more and more powerful and resourceful each time until you start to feel better. Stay in your newest TV power image until you are ready to leave it.

REVIEW

1 Multi-sensory images make strong memory traces. Their applications are described in Chapter 11. In this chapter we practise developing them.

2 The finger-thumb trigger allows you to to bring back the joy of learning into any unpleasant situation.

3 Create your own crystal study centre to minimize distractions around your study environment.

4 Use the television screen in your crystal study centre to get rid of exam or any other anxiety.

11   Doctor Lozanov's Concerts

Suggestopedia

Suggestopedia, or teaching with suggestion, grew from the work of a Bulgarian physician, psychiatrist and educational researcher, Georgi Lozanov. For over a quarter of a century he has been developing a teaching formula which helps students to understand and memorize material faster than traditional methods. It was brought to the West by Sheila Ostrander and Lynn Schroeder in their book, *Psychic Discoveries Behind the Iron Curtain*. Suggestopedia is now used in various educational institutions throughout Australia and other countries around the world. The Accelerative Learning Society of Australia has been formed to research and promote new findings in teaching and learning efficiency.

Pure suggestopedia has several different facets. The main ones in a two-lesson cycle are:

Lesson 1:   physical stretching exercises,
relaxation,
mind-calming (visualizing),
positive suggestion from the teacher,
deciphering (teaching new material),
an active concert,
a passive concert.

Lesson 2:   elaboration (using yesterday's new material).

The deciphering and elaboration components are unsuitable for individual use outside the classroom, so they are not included in this book. Affirmative action has replaced positive suggestion from the teacher, and the minute turn-ons replace the physical exercises (which in the suggestopedia class are like the ones you might do for a warm-up in the gym). Suggestopedic mind-calming is similar to the directed imagery of the last chapter. Now we come to the concerts.

Super glue for the memory

Students have described concerts as 'super glue for the memory'. Whatever you learn in a study session can be superglued into your long-term memory by the concerts. A concert is Lozanov's discovery for memorizing material that has already been learned and understood.

Concerts cannot teach anything. They cannot teach you a foreign language if you do not understand the structure of that language. They *can* help you memorize vocabulary and handy phrases for travel. They cannot teach you mathematical processes if you do not understand those processes. They *can* help you memorize them once you understand them. In the commercial world concerts are called 'Superlearning', not because they are useful in learning for understanding but because they are useful in learning for memorizing. They are excellent tools for revising and rote learning.

A concert is your spoken recording of the material you want to learn, accompanied by special music. The purpose of the music is to assist you to relax and to recruit the right hemisphere of your brain into joining your left hemisphere in the memorizing task. Using our paradigm, speech is processed by the left hemisphere, so if you played back your spoken recording of the material only your left hemisphere would be working. By playing the music the right hemisphere is also activated and recruited into helping out in the learning task.

Concerts can last from a few minutes to a few hours. A guide is to make your concert about 10 per cent of your study time. If you study for two hours, make your tape in the last 12 minutes of your session. If you have to learn a lot in a hurry you can put it onto C90 cassettes, so that each concert is up to 45 minutes long.

There are two types of concert: the active and the passive. Both are effective, but the active has limitations.

The active concert

To use the active concert you need to have a knowledge of European classical music, in particular that music which is rousing or romantic. You sing the words of the material you are learning to the same tune as the symphony or concerto or whatever you are using as music. As you sing, your voice changes and reflects the mood of the piece—sad, light, tense, strong, happy, tender, etc. As you read–sing aloud, your pace and rhythm also match the music. You distort the sound and sense of the material you are reading so that it fits right into the music. This limits its usefulness in foreign language learning where linguistic rhythm and intonation determine the meanings of words. The limitation is less in subjects where rote learning of lists, tables, hypotheses, theorems and definitions is not dependent on the rhythm of the language for their meanings. When you are reading for the active concert use the same echo-time pauses which are described in the passive concert section.

The effect of the active concert is a bit like the advertising jingle. When you think of a product that is advertised on television you will often hear in your imagination a tune that accompanies it. That is because the advertiser is using this combination of speech and music to ram into the viewer's memory the message of the product.

Among your friends and relatives you are likely to find someone who has music suitable for the active concert. Look for concerto or symphony works that are instrumental only and have no voices. Many people enjoy the works of composers such as Mozart, Beethoven, Brahms, Haydn, and

Tchaikovsky, but whatever classical music turns you on is fine.

Limitations of the active concert are:

1 You need to know the music well enough to sing it.

2 You can use each piece of music once only. After a single use it is 'filled up' with the material you have sung onto it. To use the same music again for different material causes confusion equivalent to the images of a double-exposed film negative.

3 If you are a musician you may habitually analyse the music and the musicians. This activates mainly your left hemisphere, the same one as the spoken material you are hearing—therefore your right hemisphere stays dormant. Even if you are a musician, however, you can benefit fully from the passive concert.

The passive concert

This concert is so well recognized now that it is marketed around the world as 'Superlearning'.

Whereas in the active concert learners keep their eyes open to read the material while it is being sung, in the passive concert the learner is physically passive, with eyes closed, resting and relaxing.

It is also called the pseudo-passive concert, because although the students' bodies are passive, their minds are in 'hyper-drive'. Students experience what some call 'opening up a fourth dimension to the memory banks'.

Once people have experienced the passive concert, many are not content to save the music just for the concert. Accountants play it when they are reading up on their new tax laws. Doctors play it when they are boning up on medical advances. Students play it on their Walkmans while they are listening to lectures.

Conducting your own concert

Making the tape is easiest if there is a dubbing facility on your cassette recorder. Have a copy of a cassette of passive concert music ready, and simply dub your voice over the music as you read out the material that you want to learn. As you dub, adjust the recording level so that your voice is a little stronger than the music.

If dubbing is not possible you can make the tape this way:

1 You need two cassette players.

2 Use one for playing the passive concert music.

3 Use the other to read and record what you want to remember.

That is all!

Where do you want to have your concert? In your study room, or elsewhere?

In your room

If you want to use the concert at home you play back your spoken recording on one cassette player and the music on the other cassette player, both at the same time.

Anywhere

If you want to take your concert cassette with you to play in the car or on your Walkman, you will need to have the music and the material on the same cassette. To do this, play the music on one player in the background while you are speaking and recording onto the other. In this way the music will come through as a backing to your voice. Adjust the volumes so that your voice is a little stronger than the music. Hi-fi is not of great importance as long as the sound is reasonably pleasant.

Echo time

When you are reading your work onto the cassette read in phrases or short sentences. If the sentence is long, break it up like this.

1   Study notes

Scientists claimed that nature planted billions of neurones in the brain at birth [*Pause*] but as the years passed the number of these cells diminished. [*Pause*] Some experts said that many million neurones died each day [*Pause*] never to be replaced. [*Pause*] But in 1984 came the solid experimental evidence [*Pause*] that brain cells, like all gland cells, turn over; [*Pause*] new neurones are being produced by the brain all the time. [*Pause*] From *The Fabric of Mind* [*Pause*] by the Melbourne University neurosurgeon [*Pause*] Richard Bergland.

2   English vocabulary expansion

anent—concerning, about [*Pause*]
baldric—belt passing over left shoulder to right hip for a sword or bugle. [*Pause*]
cachou—scented sweet used by smokers to disguise the odour of tobacco in the breath. [*Pause*]

3   Foreign languages

Bagaimana saya dapat kesana? [*Pause*] How do I get there? [*Pause*]
or, in reverse:
How do I get there? [*Pause*] *Bagaimana saya dapat kesana?* [*Pause*]
or the sandwich version:
Bagaimana saya dapat kesana? [*Pause*] How do I get there? [*Pause*] *Bagaimana saya dapat kesana* [*Pause*]

4   Definitions

Endochondral ossification—the replacement of cartilage by bone. [*Pause*] or:

Endochondral ossification [*Pause*]—the replacement of cartilage by bone. [*Pause*]

or:

The replacement of cartilage by bone. [*Pause*] Endochondral ossification. [*Pause*]

Your preference is the only guide you have to the arrangement of the material. Read at a comfortable rate, and speak clearly. Make each pause about the same length as the piece you have just read. The best way to do this is to read the phrase out loud, then repeat it silently to yourself before you read the next phrase. So, if the first phrase takes about five seconds, you pause for five seconds. If the next takes three seconds to read, you have a three-second pause, and so on.

The pause is to allow the echo time to take place. During echo time three things happen:

1   The information is recognized and understood (because you have learned it before the concert).

2   It is processed—the information is linked to things you already know and to any multi-sensory images you may be having.

3   It is filed in your long-term memory banks.

Multi-sensations

It is in the second step—the processing—that the skills you develop in multi-sensory imaging will be rewarded. As you are passively listening to the concert with your eyes closed, allow imagery associated with the phrases you are hearing to come into your mind. The imagery may be in any form. It may be directly connected to the work you have just learned—the colours on a map, the smell of the pages of a reference book you consulted, an emotion, such as anger generated by an author's foolish argument. It may be seemingly unconnected—the phone ringing at the start of a chapter, or you suddenly becoming aware of your knees being cold as the concert progresses.

The rule is: 'Allow and encourage any image (from any of the senses) to form while the concert is in progress, but avoid trying to forcefully create imagery. When an image comes that is fine, and if one does not that is okay too.'

As you develop multi-sensory imagery you will have more vivid and more frequent images accompanying the concert tape, and eventually you may be able to run the whole concert with hardly a break in the flow of imagery.

To recap the passive concert so far:

1   Read your notes with echo-time pauses onto tape 1.

2   Later, replay tape 1 together with concert music on tape 2.

3   While your passive concert is playing, relax, close your eyes, and allow any multi-sensations to come and go as you listen. Easy, isn't it?

Hybrid concerts

There is a variation students sometimes use. When the notes they are learning are dense or complex they prepare a hybrid concert. First they re-read their notes while they are listening to the passive concert of those notes, and after that they do step 3.

The most logical time to do the step 1 recording is in the final few minutes of your last study session for the day. Five to ten minutes' recording should be enough each day. You might like to make a tape for each different unit, and add a new segment each time you do further study in that unit.

In steps 2 and 3, the replaying, relaxing and imaging take place straight after your home-made physical relaxation tape as you prepare for each new study session.

If you have combined the music and the spoken notes together you can play the cassette anywhere—in the car, in the kitchen, commuting, in the library. It is not always necessary for you to be physically relaxed when you play it, although that is the time when the concert has its strongest effect. You can play the cassette over and over, but if you relax before you listen it is really only necessary to play it

- the day after you recorded it,
- a week after you recorded it,
- a month after you recorded it,
- at the end of the term,
- before the exam.

Passive concert music

The reason for the music is to help you relax and to recruit your right brain into the memorizing session. The passive concert music is more relaxing than that used in the active concert. You can use any gentle music that has no surprises—no crashing crescendos or moody dramatics in it. You may call it 'boring' music, and that is a handy description—pleasant and boring. If it plods along in four-four time at a rate of around fifty to sixty beats per minute that is fine. Any pleasant wind or string instruments such as the violin, harpsichord, organ, flute, mandolin, or guitar, are all okay. Look for any largo music from the classical baroque composers such as the Bachs (J. S., J. C., W. F., or C. P. S.), Corelli, Handel, Telemann, Vivaldi.

Lozanov talks of the 'golden harmonies' of the classical baroque composers, and insists that only this music is effective. That may be so in Europe. In Australia any gentle pleasant regular music produces the hypermnesic (super-memory) effect. One of the popular cassettes I use for the passive concert has no deliberate harmonies, no four-four time, no fixed number of beats per minute and is not baroque. It is a continuously improvised melody of delicate synthesized piano sounds.

Baroque largo music works with people of all nationalities and ages, and so does pleasant gentle boring music from non-European cultures around the world.

On the other hand, you may find it reassuring to start by making your own concerts with the official Superlearning music cassette, available from Personal Development, 60 Dixon Drive, Holder, ACT 2611.

Unlike the active concert where an orchestral piece can only be used once, the same music can be used again and again in the passive concert. I like to record a piece such as Pachelbel's Canon repeatedly on both sides of a C90 cassette tape, so that I can tape material for as long as I want to.

If you research further into the idea of active and passive concerts you will find all kinds of theories about how they should be organized. One version of the passive concert is that you have to fit the reading of your notes into time segments precisely four seconds long, followed by precisely four seconds of pause—you can even buy a timer tape to measure the times. Echo time works just as well, and is easier to manage.

Various versions of the passive concert also place emphasis on correct breathing:
• inhale before you start reading the next phrase,
• hold your breath while you are reading,
• exhale and inhale before you start again.
Once again, special breathing is not necessary.

Some concerteers insist that when the concert is being read, it must be spoken in a cycle of three different 'tones': the first phrase gentle, the second medium, the third authoritative, the fourth gentle, etc. Reading normally with echo time works just as well.

Your turn

Take some time off now from reading to see if you have any music suitable for the passive concert. If you do, make a concert tape by reading through all the review sections at the end of each chapter in this book. (Yes, you can even include in your concert the reviews of chapters you have not yet read!)

Then sit down, relax, and enjoy your first concert.

REVIEW

1   The active concert (of limited use)
Recording:
- Sing your material onto the tape to match the mood of the classical romantic music.
- Use echo time—roughly equal times each for speech and pause.

Listening:
- Play it back at any time.
- Follow the written notes with your eyes open.

2   The passive concert
Recording:
- Use gentle, regular, pleasant, relaxing music with no surprises or changes.
- Make your voice slightly louder than the music.
- Use echo time for pauses.
- Record at the end of your daily study session.

Listening:
- Play the passive concert tape after your relaxation tape, and before you start each new study session.
- When you have developed relaxation skill, dispense with the relaxation tape and use the passive concert instead for your pre-study relaxation.
- Listen to the concert as though it were a real concert—enjoy it!
- Let any multi-sensations develop in your mind, and blend them with the concert material.

Playing passive concert music softly in the background helps concentration and comprehension when you are studying.

12 The Warm-up

Back in Chapter 5 in the three-day time budget there was an item called pre-study which took about nine minutes to do. The pre-study exercises or the warm-up guarantee that you will have high productivity in any 'head work' activity you are about to do, regardless of whether it is going to take one hour or five hours to complete.

For reading, planning, preparation, study, writing, targeting, research, for anything that needs prolonged concentration, the warm-up is the best way to start. As you have read the preceding chapters you can do almost all of the warm-up already. Here are a few more pointers.

Using the warm-up

1 Drink your glass of water and make your affirmation

Drink the water mouthful by mouthful, instead of down-the-hatch. This is a convenient time to do affirmative action. As you take each sip repeat any affirmations you are working on. Imagine you are putting them into each sip of water, and as you swallow pretend they are being infused right into the very centre of your being.

2 Do your turn-ons, acupoints and tension easers

Remember that they have a cumulative effect, and they become more useful the more often you use them.

3 Relax to your concert tape

At first you will play your home-made mind-clearing and multi-sensory imagery tapes to lead into your most recent concert. After a while, when you are experiencing some multi-sensations in your concert, there is no need for the mind-clearing and multi-sensory imagery—the concert will do the mind-clearing for you, and the concert will also provide your practice in multi-sensory imagery!

4 Pen-power for the goal and the time

What easy short term-goal are you going to achieve this session? Are you going to finish the chapter? start planning the essay? do a bit more art? Whatever you think you can finish easily, write it down. Use pen-power and write it down somewhere—anywhere!

Write down how long you want to study before your first break.

Package your time attractively. Do you want a break after 40 minutes? After 60 minutes? If you work in 60 minute slots and it is 7.40 a.m. when you commence, write 8.40 a.m. beside your notes. For variety, use a kitchen timer, and set it to ring after 60 minutes.

When you have done each hour, *reward* yourself by getting up for a drink of water and doing a few turn-ons, or eating some fruit or a biscuit. Avoid the television, because two minutes of television watching has an amazing ability to take up a whole hour.

After a short break go back to your desk, and do the pen-power targeting and timing for the next study session.

5　Fast-forward Targeting

Fast-forward yourself to the end of the study session by imagining you have finished the session you are now about to commence. Imagine you have achieved the target you have just written down in number 4. For 15 seconds tune into your body, and notice how it feels to pretend your study session has already been successful.

REVIEW

The whole warm-up time takes the time of your concert, plus a couple of minutes in total for the other items.

1　Drink a glass of water, and make your affirmations.

2　Spend a minute or two on some turn-ons, acupoints and tension easers.

3　Relax, and enjoy your most recent concert.

4　Use pen-power with your goal for this session and the time for this session.

5　Fast-forward targeting: imagine for fifteen seconds how it feels to have achieved your study goal.

13   Reading Strategies

The first part of *Superstudy* has described the warm-up exercises, the reasons for their use, and why it is worthwhile starting off the first minutes of every major study session with them. Now we can move into the second part of this book, which covers the learning session. You will be given techniques that are useful when you are learning new information or doing assignments.

The overview

After doing the warm-up exercises you already know what you want to accomplish during the learning session. The warm-up has turned on both the left and right hemispheres, and they are ready for action. The first thing to do is to make use of the holistic function of your right hemisphere. It will enable you to work directly towards your target if you give it an overview of the work you want to complete. It will warn you when you start straying into non-productive areas by saying, 'Hey, is this relevant to your topic?'

What you do in the overview depends on your target for the session.

- Is it notetaking? Then glance through the headings of the books, journals, etc., you are going to take notes from.
- Is it writing an essay? Then keep in mind the topic you have chosen to write on, and scan through your notes.
- Is it maths problems? Briefly review the mathematical principles on which the problems are based.

The sixty seconds you spend on this scanning will give you an overview which will allow your right hemisphere to help your understanding and direction during the whole study session.

Having completed the overview, you are now in the learning session proper.

Reading smarter not longer

The average tertiary student spends more time on researching and writing essays than anything else. Your lecturers may have rigid specifications for the way in which essays are to be done—depart from these at your peril! However, there is an unwritten rule that often applies to the marks awarded to essays. It is this: 'The bigger the bibliography the higher the marks.'

What is a bibliography? The old definition is: 'A list of books read in order to write an essay.' The new definition for you is this: 'A list of books consulted in order to write an essay.' By changing the single word 'read' to 'consult' you can save 50 per cent of the time usually needed for researching an essay. Here is how it works.

Indexed essays

When an essay topic is set, the lecturer usually provides a reading list with it. Conscientious students rush for the library, grab the books and start reading from cover to cover, trying to ingest a lot of information—including plenty which they will later find to be irrelevant.

The most efficient way to tackle the essay has nine simple steps.

1 Take the key words of the essay topic, and look them up in the encyclopaedia and a dictionary. This gives the right-brain an overview which will keep you on track while collecting information. The *Encyclopaedia Britannica* should be avoided because of its dense style; it is easier to use encyclopaedias which are more simply written—such as those for children—which contain the same information as the *Britannica* but are easier to read and faster to use.

2 Look at the suggested reading list for the essay. Find the locations of these books in the library shelves.

3 Look along the shelf on either side of each book to find similar books on the same subject.

4 Take note of the key words of the essay again, and look them up in the index of all the books in that area.

5 Every time you find a few lines or paragraphs that are relevant to the essay topic, read the information a few times until you understand it, then close the book and write down the idea in your own words, together with the details of the book (title, author, etc.).

6 Looking up the key words in the subject catalogue also reveals different places in the library shelves where books can be plundered for their indexes. Enjoy the search. Pretend you are a pirate looking for buried treasures!

7 Before long you will have flipped through twenty or thirty books and the relevant information will start to recur from one book to another. That signals it is time to stop.

8 Finally, scan through the basic reference books the lecturer suggested and ensure that you have information on all the main points of the topic.

9 Now you are ready to write the essay:
   • start with an unexpected or controversial statement from one of the books (to get the lecturer's attention);
   • link all your notes from the various books;
   • finish with a broad summary of your argument, and then state your own beliefs about the topic.

Doing essays this way is fun. And how erudite they look with all those references in the bibliography!

More reading secrets

There are times when it is unwise to avoid compulsory reading. For example, you may be requested to lead a tutorial in which a particular book is dissected and analysed. Here are some useful tactics for intensive reading.

1 First and final

To use this read the first and last sections and sub-sections of the material to be studied.

If it is a journal article, read:
- the first and final paragraphs of the article,
- the first and final sentences of each paragraph.

If it is a book, read:
- the entire first and final chapters,
- the first and final paragraphs of all other chapters,
- and for more detail read the first and final sentences of each paragraph in each chapter.

This is holistic right-hemisphere reading. You get about 80 per cent of the material for about 20 per cent of the labour. Not a bad dividend!

2 Question-izing

This means turning any headings into questions, and reading as if you wanted to find an answer to those questions. The effect of looking for an answer draws your concentration strongly to the content under the headings. Take Chapter 1 as an example. The first sub-heading would change to this:

'The Need to Fail'—Who needs to fail?
or The need to fail what?
or Do I need to fail?
and so on.

Sometimes there will be answers to the questions and sometimes there will not. It makes no difference either way. Finding the answer is not important, only the process is important because it helps you to concentrate on what you are reading, and changes the task into a game.

3 Doubling-up

If the material to be read is written in a condensed 'academic' style so that it cannot be easily understood, use the doubling-up technique. After briefly scanning the chapter and looking at any pictures, diagrams and cartoons, turn the heading into a question, and then read through the first paragraph. Then read the first paragraph again. Then read the second; then re-read the second. Then the third, re-read it, and so on, as far as necessary, re-reading every paragraph immediately. For really turgid texts, the techniques of first and final, turning headings into questions and doubling-up, can all be used at the same time.

4 Eye-speed reading

Even when the material being read is quite easy to understand, many people slow down their natural reading rate by habitually glancing back over what they have just read. To eliminate this habit simply hold a cardboard mask or a piece of paper on the book *above* the line you are now reading so that it covers the previous lines. Slide it down the page as you finish reading each new line. If you wish you can encourage yourself to speed-read by sliding the mask down a little faster than usual. This not only trains you to avoid back-tracking but also may improve your ability to remember the information you are reading.

Looking at every word you read also slows you down. While using the mask, start to focus on small groups of words, say two or three at a time, on the line you are reading. Then increase the size of the word groups to four or five or more until after a while you have trained your eyes to alight on only a couple of places in each entire line. In the process you may discover that you are no longer 'talking silently to yourself' when you read—you are getting the meaning directly from the page to your mind without having to go through your inner voice. With practice you can realize your natural potential to read, and you will be able to comprehend over a thousand words a minute using this method!

REVIEW

1 Overview
Start with a one-minute overview of the material you want to cover in the learning session.

2 Indexed essays
(a) Get an overview of the essay topic from a children's encyclopaedia.
(b) Look up the key words of the essay in the subject catalogue in the library.
(c) Check nearby books in each of the different areas of the shelves.
(d) Flip through the books, doing an index search.
(e) Take the details of each book which has something to say on your topic, and write its message in your own words. Details of all relevant books go into your bibliography.
(f) Finally, check the books your lecturer has recommended.
(g) Write the essay, starting with a controversial statement, and ending with a summary and a statement of your own beliefs.

3 More reading tricks
(a) First and final—read the first and last segments.
(b) Question-izing—turn headings into questions.
(c) Doubling-up—read every paragraph twice.
(d) Eye-speed reading—use a mask to avoid back-tracking, and group words when reading.

14 Einstein and Beyond

Who was the greatest thinker of our time? Would you agree that Einstein was up there with the best? What a marvellous brain he had! Do you ever wish you had a brain like his?

Your wish has been granted. You do have a brain like his! If the brain of Einstein and your brain and anyone else's brain were all displayed on the same table it would be impossible to tell whose was whose. The reason for Einstein's ability was not in his brain but in the way he used it.

He left evidence of how he used his thinking in letters he wrote to friends. In these he told how his imagination was the key to his fantastic discoveries. To learn the secrets of the universe Einstein fantasized that he became the various elements that he was investigating. For example, when examining gravitation he imagined what it was like to be objects caught in the gravity force field. He once pretended that he was in a lift that was free-falling down a long elevator shaft. How would his body feel, he fantasized, and what would he see around him? How would the free-fall affect the way his muscles moved his body? Would there be any difference if the temperature changed, or the light? Then he would pretend to be an object in the pocket of the falling man. How would it feel to be the chain on the man's key-ring? Becoming the chain, what sensations would he notice around him? What could he hear, smell or taste? Einstein would have asked questions like these in his search for understanding of the other elements.

Do the questions sound familiar to you? Does it remind you of multi-sensory imagery? Yes, it is another payoff for your practice of Chapter 10.

Elemental learning

In your learning session take a tip from Einstein. Use your multi-sensory imagery to become an element of what you are learning. If, say, you are studying the role of the hypothalamus and its relationship to the sympathetic and parasympathetic divisions of the autonomic nervous system, develop your multi-sensory images and become the hypothalamus, then become the sympathetic division and the parasympathetic division, and then become the whole autonomic nervous system. Finally, become everything simultaneously—the hypothalamus and its effect on the sympathetic and parasympathetic divisions of the autonomic nervous system.

Or, to take an easier example, I pretend I am learning Pythagoras' theorem: 'In any right-angled triangle the square on the hypotenuse is equal to the sum of the squares of the other two sides.'

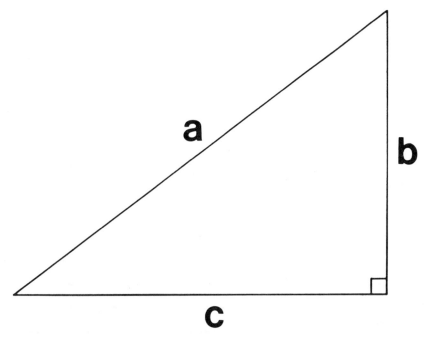

I become the hypotenuse, and fantasize, 'I am the hypotenuse'. I feel tense and tight like the bowstring stretched over a bow. My job is to contain B and C—without me they would keep shooting away forever from each other and from our right angle. My imaginary colour is yellow, and my taut surface is very smooth. I smell like twine. I feel distant from the right-angle home of B and C. I feel sad that I can never be a part of their origin. And I know that my square is equal to both of theirs put together.

I could also become other elements of this theorem:

I am side B: I feel . . .

I am side C: I feel . . .

I am the right angle: I feel . . .

I am the plane: I feel . . .

I am the area: I feel . . .

I am the complete triangle: I feel . . .

If I became all of these, $A^2 = B^2 + C^2$ would suffer from multi-sensory overkill. Just one or two of the elements is sufficient. I have chosen this example, to illustrate how almost anything you want to learn can be indelibly imprinted in your memory using this method. There is no 'correct' way to do the imagery. If you were to do Pythagoras's theorem your images would be completely different from mine. Just let your imagination have free rein.

Because the description above is written, it may seem long and arduous. In reality it is a brief technique lasting only a few seconds, and it does not need to be recorded in any way—the multi-sensory imagery you generate will make it live for you indefinitely.

Your turn

Look around you and let your eyes alight on an object. Imagine you are a single element of that object. Perhaps the design on a cup or the felt tip of a highlighter pen. Become the element, and describe yourself using your multi-sensory imagination.

The element I choose to become is _____

My colour is _____

I feel _____

My movement is _____

The pressure on me is _____

The tastes around me are _____

I smell _____

I hear _____

When it is dark I _____

What else? _____

_____

_____

Beyond Einstein

Einstein's method can be improved and developed one step further. He often used muscular movements when he was investigating the elements of his fantasies. This made use of the learning ability of his body so that it could supplement the learning ability of his brain.

In his book, *The Fabric of Mind* (Penguin, Ringwood, Vic., 1985, p. 109), Melbourne University neurosurgeon Richard Bergland asks the question, 'Can thinking go on outside the brain?' His answer is a definite YES! His research shows that the process of thought is spread right throughout the body in hormones, and, every time we move, these hormones act on the brain. When this happens we learn. Intelligence is in the body as well as the brain.

Bergland and other brain researchers are beginning to provide evidence for what parents and teachers have known for ages: the best way to make sure children know something is to ask them to do it physically. Even the learning of an abstract concept is more powerful if children use their bodies to understand it rather than just their brains. To help children solve personal problems, child psychologists give them dolls to play with or a sandpit to play in. When school learning starts, teachers guide the children to play with counters and blocks of wood as they begin to learn the theory of mathematics and other abstractions. Unfortunately the longer a student is at school the more this fundamental learning procedure is overlooked. In my eight years of tertiary study all the lecturers ever used my body for was to mark me present if my bottom was on a seat. What a waste of body intelligence!

Embodiment

This means getting the learning into the body. In accelerative learning workshops and classes nowadays the desks have been thrown out because the learners never sit still long enough to use them. Most of their learning is done through the body. It is more effective than learning through the mere intellect of the brain.

Embodiment is the logical extension of Einstein's method. Whatever you are studying you can find a way to move your body in some way to mimic an element in the topic you are learning. If you are learning shorthand put some old shoes on and shuffle-draw the marks with your feet in earth or sand. If you are learning steel production in science, draw the outline of a furnace in chalk on your bedroom carpet (it comes off after a while!), and become the iron ore. Pretend you are being pummelled and roasted as you enter the furnace. Imagine what it would feel/smell/sound/taste/look like, as you become transformed by the heat from rough pig-iron into beautiful high-grade steel. As you exit through the base of your chalk-drawn furnace imagine how you are drawn out into appropriate lengths and cooled.

Micro-muscle movement

Embodiment can be used anywhere. It is acceptable to move your body in subjects designated as 'practical' (food science, lab work, physical education, manual arts, drama, etc.). And you can do anything you like in the privacy of your own room. But what about using embodiment in the traditional sit-down-and-shut-up lesson?

In this situation use micro-muscle movement. Instead of getting out of your seat and performing the large-scale physical motion you would normally use to accelerate your learning, scale down your body movements until they become so small that they are almost invisible.

For example, practise walking without changing your body position as you read this paragraph. Do it now. Feel your muscles move inside each leg in turn, even though anyone looking at you could not detect a thing because your legs are hardly moving on the outside. You can involve every part of your body in micro-muscle movement. It is just as effective as embodiment using total body motion, and it is even more fun because nobody knows you are doing it.

Micro-muscle movement can be used in any subject with a little imagination. You only have to do it once, and it will be imprinted in your memory for as long as you need it. Give your brain a rest regularly by using the intelligence of your body. Remember that while your body is moving, your mind cannot remain stuck.

REVIEW

1 Elemental learning
To understand and remember indelibly, select an element, and become that element using your multi-sensory imagery.

2 Embodiment
Incorporate your body into what you are learning. Move it. Feel it. Imitate it. Dance it.

3 Micro-muscle movement
Use the scaled-down version of embodiment when you want people to be unaware of how you are learning.

15 Your Preferred Learning Mode

'Use your body as a learning instrument!' is also the cry of the new-mind technology known as Neuro-linguistic Programming, NLP for short. Researchers John Grinder and Richard Bandler made a significant discovery in the 1970s which has enabled people to learn better and faster. Their findings concern the ways in which people receive and process information from the environment. The question the researchers sought to answer was 'Does everybody perceive and process information in the same way?' Learning can also be described as the perception and processing of information, so another way of putting the question is 'Does everybody learn the same way?'

They found that in any group of people it is rare for everyone to learn the same way. Except for some of the disabled, people can see, hear, feel, taste and smell easily enough. Most of us, however, are not continually aware of the information we are getting through our senses of taste and smell. Think of the scents or aromas in the air you are breathing now, or of the taste in your mouth—were you aware of these before you started this paragraph?

You are usually aware, to a greater or lesser degree, of what you can see, hear or feel around you. Obviously you can see the words you are reading, you can hear things around you (an air-conditioner, or traffic, or birds), and you can feel the clothing against your skin. Whilst you are aware of these three modes of perception you do not rely on them equally to gain knowledge from the environment. Some people interpret the world around them mainly through their eyes. NLP terms them 'Visuals'. Some get most of their information through their ears. They are the 'Auditories'. Of the others, most prefer to feel their way through this earthly journey—they are the 'Kinesthetics'.

A few years ago I was driving near Bellingen, north of Sydney, when I saw a petrol station blow up. Miraculously nobody was hurt, even though there were people in and around the place when it happened. Traffic to Coffs Harbour was held up for hours, so I talked with some of the other drivers. 'Jeez, mate! You shoulda seen the fireball! Looked brighter than an atom bomb!' said one. 'It was pandemonium. Everyone was shouting and screaming, and the roar of the flames was deafening', said his companion. 'Yeah, well, I just finished putting air in me tyres when this wall of heat hit me fair in the face. Well, I jumped in the ute and backed out like a bullet', said a third.

All three of them were at the same place at the same time. They all experienced the same incident and yet they spoke as if they were in three

different worlds. Can you pick the Visual? The Auditory? The Kinesthetic? The words that are used in speech are not random. They reflect the way each person takes in and gives out information.

- A Visual appears comfortable communicating about his visual world in visual vocabulary—see, clear, watch, appear, sight, looks, focus, brighter, show, view—these and hundreds of other visual words will be used much more often than words of sounds or feelings.
- When you feel that someone is using lots of words about touch or motion or feelings—warm, thrill, feel, firm, solid, grab, grasp, excited, putting, hit, jumped, backed out, etc.—you are listening to a Kinesthetic.
- An Auditory speaks with a higher proportion of hearing words—sing, listen, sounds, talk, discuss, hear, loud, says, pandemonium, shout, scream, roar, deafen.

See-ers, listeners and doers

As well as the types of words you use, there are other indicators which reflect your preferred mode of perception.

See-ers

Visual people frequently move their eyes above the horizontal. Their voices are high-pitched, and they speak quickly, gulping in air between sentences for their shallow breathing high up in the chest. Commentators of fast action sports (football, horse racing, swimming, athletics) are often Visuals because they have the ability to see, interpret and comment on the swiftly changing positions of the players and competitors. Visual people are aware of how they look, and they dress more for appearance than comfort.

Listeners

The eyes of Auditories move mainly horizontally to the left and right, and also down to their non-dominant hand (not the one they write with). They have moderate pleasant voices, and breathe at a normal rate into their mid-chest region. The head and feet are neither forward nor backward, but if they were horses they would be sway-backed because their tummies protrude (whether they have a beer gut or not) and the buttocks stick out at the back. They often have their hands around their ears, touching them or fiddling with nearby hair, or the palms face each other in the position of 'Let me tell you about the fish I caught that was this big!' An Auditory is rarely without a radio or cassette playing nearby. An Auditory would rather buy the latest album to listen to repeatedly, whereas a Visual prefers to spend the money on buying a ticket to see the group in concert.

Doers

The eyes of Kinesthetics often look down to the side in the direction of the dominant hand. The voice is slow, deep and breathy, like the sexy sound of a late-night radio announcer. They breathe like yogis, taking the air down deeply, slowly in and slowly out. Their bodies are thickset, with a low centre of gravity, because they want to get as close to the earth as their bodies allow. They love nature and doing things with their hands, so they manifest as earthy people—perhaps the earth mother or the farmer or the mechanic. Kinesthetics refuse to wear uncomfortable clothing, no matter how smart it may look. When they walk their feet precede their body. They want their feet to feel what the environment is like before they bring the rest of their body into it.

It is fun to assess your relatives and friends. You will find that many of them fit so neatly into the Visual, Auditory or Kinesthetic types that you wonder how they could possibly be unaware of it. If your lecturers or teachers are Visuals and you are also a Visual, you will have a natural rapport. If you are an Auditory or a Kinesthetic, then use the descriptions above to model the Visuals and use lots of visual words when you are talking to them. Similarly, you can model Auditory or Kinesthetic lecturers with your body and your speech. Good rapport with lecturers and teachers leads to better marks in their subjects.

You may want to stop and think about your least favourite teachers at this point. Are those teachers 'bad' because they are, for example, highly visual and teach through books and videos, while you are highly auditory and learn through talking and listening rather than reading and watching? Any other modal mismatch between you and a teacher is also throwing up a challenge for your learning. Identify your strong mode, and find out what you can do with it.

Discovering your mode

If you are not sure yet which is your preferred mode, grab a cassette recorder and a stopwatch or egg-timer, and do this exercise.

Imagine you are making a letter cassette tape to send to me. On it you are telling me about a special place where you enjoy being. When you have chosen the place:

1   Set the timer for exactly three minutes, and describe to me without pausing the things I would *see* if I were there with you.

2   Set the timer again for three minutes, and tell me all the things I might expect to *hear* if I was with you at your special place.

3   Set the timer for another three minutes, and tell me what I could touch or *feel*, or what emotions I might have about the place.

Using your mode

You will have found that one of these modes was more difficult than the others, and one was easier than the others. The one that was easiest is your preferred mode.

If it was the first, then you prefer the visual mode. The most efficient way you process information is by seeing it. You find studying relatively easy because written information is your strength—but you may get a blockage when you are writing assignments because writing is a kinesthetic activity. A tactic to overcome this is to visualize your next paragraph already written on the next blank part of the page, and then copy what you imagine you see. You can utilize your visual strength by watching relevant study videos and films, by sticking your notes up on the wall, and any other ways of getting information through your eyes.

If the second three minutes was easiest for you, auditory learning is your best way. Study efficiency for you lies in playing enjoyably relaxing 'Super-learning' tapes or soft ABC–FM music while you are working. Having regular concerts is important. When appropriate, work in a study or tutorial group and sound out your ideas with other group members. If you know in advance that you have to miss a lecture, ask someone to record it for you.

If the third way was easiest for you, you are probably kinesthetically oriented, and learning by doing is your best way. Participate in all practical lessons and workshops. The minute turn-ons and the Yin–Yang exercises are immediately helpful. Get moving into elemental learning and embodiment as much as possible in everything you learn. Increase the intensity of your emotions when you are doing multi-sensory imagery.

The nutcracker

Regardless of which is your preferred mode, if you are finding a subject a tough nut to crack, get into it with all three modes:
- read it, view it, watch it, use colour in your notes, etc., for the visual mode;
- tape it, listen to it, discuss it, read it aloud, etc., for the auditory mode;
- embody it, imagine its elements, move it, dance it, use multi-sensory imagery on it, write it, involve your body in it in order to feel it.

Efficient study or self-education?

You have a value judgement to make here. Whilst it is more efficient for you to learn in your preferred mode, the more you rely on it the weaker your other modes become. The ideal is eventually to go for balance over all three modes. Although the efficiency of utilizing your preferred mode will get you there in the short term, it is important to keep educating your less preferred modes for the long term by learning material through them. Only you can decide when to go for efficiency and when to go for self-education. One solution is to learn in your preferred mode when under pressure from deadlines, and to use the others in times of 'plain sailing'.

Presentations

When it is your turn to give a tutorial or lead a seminar topic, remember to cater for the different processing modes of the group. Prepare your information in visual, auditory and kinesthetic modes. In other words, as you talk about the topic give the Visuals something to look at, such as a map or diagram or graph. Supplement this by involving everyone's bodies in some way—perhaps hand around a sample product for inspection after your talk, or put a question to them and ask them to write down their thoughts, or ask them to stand up and move away into small groups for a brief discussion, or suggest they close their eyes and imagine they are physically involved in an element of your presentation.

Excelling in spelling

Is your spelling good? No? Then you are probably sounding out the words to yourself when you are writing them down. Another NLP discovery is that excelling in spelling is a visual activity, not an auditory one. If you are an Auditory sounding out your letters, how do you learn to spell visually? Easy. Become a Visual while you are spelling:

1   Get a good dictionary and find a challenging word (e.g. accommodation).

2   Copy the word correctly onto a sheet of paper, and then close the dictionary.

3   Stare at the word you have written. Focus on a letter at or near the centre of the word ('o'). Close and open your eyes as many times as you like until you can see the letter 'o' clearly in your mind's eye with your eyes closed.

4   Now add more letters, first to the left ('mmo') until you see the three letters with your eyes closed; then to the right ('mmodat') until you can see these with closed eyes; then to the left again ('accommodat') and finally see the whole word ('accommodation') in your mind's eye. Avoid sounding out the letters; just take a silent mental snapshot.

5   Turn your sheet over, and write the word on the back in pencil.

6   Check back over the page to make sure it is correct. If not, rub out the wrong bit with an eraser and go back to step 3.

Do this whenever you recognize that you have made a mistake in spelling. After a few dozen words your spelling mode will automatically become visual, and spelling for you will be much less of a worry.

REVIEW

1   Find out if you are an Auditory, a Visual or a Kinesthetic.

2   For fast learning use your preferred mode.

3   For heavy slogging use all three modes.

4   If you lead a tutorial, present your material to the group in all three modes.

5   Take a mental snapshot of spelling words.

16   Natty Notes

Here is another system which is so easy and so obvious that you will wonder why it is not yet taught as far back as primary schools for students to use throughout their learning careers. It can be used in various ways, and the main areas are organic notes, essay writing and creative writing.

Tatty notes

Do you have trouble taking notes in lectures? If you are the average student your notepad will end up as a tatty list of phrases and sentences, line after line down the page, which do not make much sense when you come to revise them a few weeks later. Develop the simple skills of organic notes to increase your notetaking efficiency.

Organic notes

1   Buy a ream of A4 blank copying or duplicating paper. The back of used computer sheets is okay for organic notes, though it is a bit hard to handle these in confined spaces such as student desks. Blank paper is necessary, and you only use one side of it. If lined paper is used your left brain will get too involved and stifle the process. Also get one of those fat little four-colour ballpoint pens or a set of fine-line fibre-tipped pens so that you have the choice of different colours. You will also need a punch, and a file.

2   Punch the file holes in one of the long sides. Turn your paper so that these will always be at the top of your organic notes.

3   When the lecture starts, write the topic in the centre of the sheet. This is the holistic patch of fertile earth from which the tree trunks, branches and foliage of notes will grow as the lecture progresses.

4   When the first main subtopic is mentioned, write it near the topic. This is one of the trunks of the trees that will grow from the earth-topic. Near here are written the notes about the sub-topic and they form the branches and foliage.

5   When the next major subtopic is mentioned you can decide whether it is closely related to the first sub-topic. If it is, start another tree near the first. If it is not, put it further away—perhaps on the opposite side of the main topic.

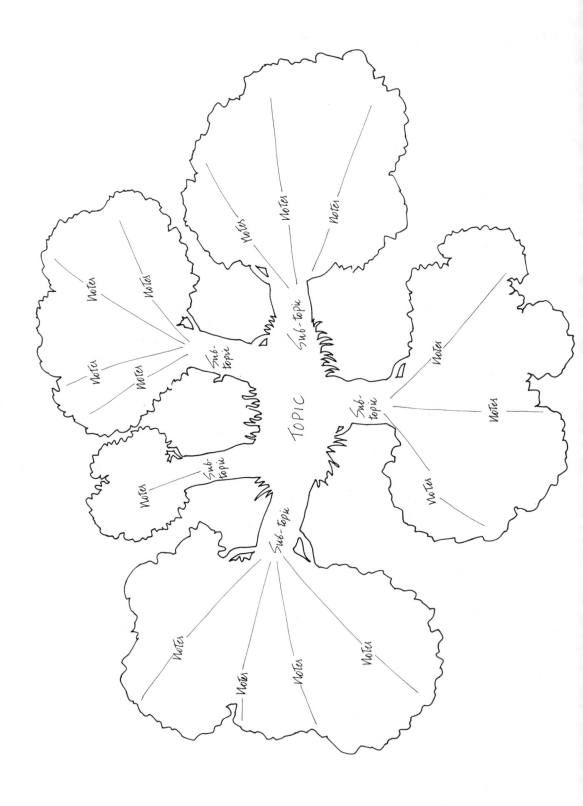

NATTY NOTES

Essays
- Record relevant information onto each blank sheet.
- Write a key word from essay topic onto each blank sheet of paper.
- Sort out the order you want for your essay.
- Write it following the style for Indexed Essays.

Mnemonics
- Relate the sentence to the topic if possible.
- Use multi-sensory imagery to enliven the sentence.
- Retrieve the key words by recalling the sentence.
- Make a ridiculous sentence using initials of key words.
- Link key words.

Subliminal Learning
- Use BluTack

Creative Writing
- Write the main idea in the centre of the page.
- Ask the topic what it wants to know or tell.
- When you have plenty to write about comes out the unsuitable bits.
- Write down quickly and unenvincically around the topic whatever comes to mind, no matter how silly or seemingly irrelevant.

Organic Notes
- Get consentina file.
- Use blank sheets lengthwise.
- Write topic in centre.
- Write sub-topics near topic and write notes towards edge of page.
- Use simple illustrations and different colour.
- Draw a wriggly border around it.
- Put on wall for a week for subliminal learning.
- Review after 1 month by summarizing into linear form.
- Review organic notes and linear notes before exam.

6   When you are writing the notes, turn it into a game by sketching simple little pictures, cartoons, graphs or maps to illustrate the notes. This will also keep your right brain tuned in to the lecture, as well as your left. With your coloured pens write the notes of each sub-topic in different colours.

7   In subsequent lessons, if the lecturer gives more information on these topics you can add them in the vacant areas next to the appropriate notes.

8   When a topic is finished draw a leafy border, or any other kind of border, around each sub-topic. At this stage it begins to look like a garden and it is from here that it gets the name organic notes.

9   Read the organic notes onto your concert tape as soon as possible—no more than two days after the lecture.
     At home during the next weekend write the date on your organic notes, and stick them to the wall, to the back of the toilet door, or somewhere else where you will see them every day for a week.
     After a week put the organic notes into a concertina file labelled 'One-month Revision'. The concertina file should have the numbers 1 to 31 on the divisions, so you can file your notes under today's date.

10 A month later revise your notes by briefly summarizing the notes in the traditional linear, down-the-page format, listing only the topics and sub-topics, and a few key phrases from the notes.
     Attach the linear notes to the organic notes and transfer them from the one-month revision file to another file labelled 'Exam Revision'.

Organic notes are similar to a process which the mnemonist Tony Buzan calls 'mind mapping'. The process increases the amount you remember. Think of a road map. When you want to drive from your place to a new destination, no matter how complex the route, all you need to do is glance at the road map for a few seconds, take a mental photograph of the route, and off you go, without having to constantly stop and recheck. A year later if you want to go to that place again you will remember how to get there without having to check the map. Your mind has an amazing ability to remember information in the organic or map form. Organic notes are a way of using this same visual process to your advantage. Some people dislike taking lecture notes this way. They take normal linear notes during the lecture, and then convert them to organic notes soon after.

Subliminal learning

In point 9 above it is suggested you stick your organic notes to a wall where you can see them every day. Once you have put them up you need not conscientiously read through them every day. Just glancing at them a few times a day is sufficient. Having them somewhere in the periphery of your visual field while you are studying is ideal—perhaps on the wall right in front of you or a little to either side of your desk. Peripheral perception is the path to using your faculty of subliminal learning, where the information goes directly into the long-term memory banks without you being aware of it.

Because of its power, this process has been banned in advertising in many countries, so in its beneficial aspect it must be worth using. For this reason it is better to have vital, peaceful, amusing or healthy pictures around your walls, rather than negative cartoons with captions such as 'Thank God it's Friday' or 'I am a prisoner of an educational institution'.

If you have any of the latter, replace them with your own affirmative action statements that you have decorated a little, or perhaps symbols that you have received from your 'guide within' or from your dreams.

As well as this type of visual subliminal learning, many people find that subliminal audio cassettes are useful in helping to develop positive attitudes to study. That is an area you might like to experiment with.

Mnemonics

Here is something that fits in very well with natty noting. Mnemonics will be a great help to you once you know how to use them. This is how.

1   As you are making organic notes or memorizing some work, find the main words of the subject you have been learning. Use the review of Chapter 12, The Warm-up, as an example:
    (a) Drink a glass of water and make your affirmations (key words: water and affirmations).
    (b) Spend a minute or two on some turn-ons, acupoints and tension easers (key words: turn-ons, acupoints and tension easers).
    (c) Relax and enjoy your most recent concert (key word: concert).
    (d) Use pen-power with your goal for this session and the time for this session (key words: goal and time).
    (e) Fast-forward targeting. Imagine for fifteen seconds how it feels to have achieved your study goal (key word: fast forward).
    The key words for the warm-up are therefore Water, Affirmations, Turn-ons, Acupoints, Tension easers, Concert, Goal, Time, Fast-forward, giving the initial letters W, A, T, A, T, C, G, T, F.

2   Now concoct a sentence which incorporates these letters in order and preferably has something to do with the topic—in this case 'The Warm-up'. A sentence is: 'We All Tremble About Terribly Cold Giraffes to Feed.' Because the sentence is so stupid and ridiculous it is easy to remember.

3   Make the sentence even more unforgettable by using multi-sensory imagery. See the whole class dressed in colourful winter clothes. You are all carrying heavy bundles of leaves to feed the giraffes. But the weather is so cold that even in your warm clothes you are trembling. See everyone trembling. Imagine you are trembling with cold yourself; hear everyone's teeth chattering, and hear them all saying 'Brrrrr!' Smell the cut leaves you are carrying, and the animal smells of the zoo. Look at the poor giraffes. They have no protection against the weather and they

are terribly cold. In fact they are so cold they are all blue, and they have icicles hanging from their heads and tails. Because they are so cold they need lots of food to stay alive . . .

In the organic notes near the part you want to memorize, write this silly sentence, and draw a simple sketch of this crazy scene.

4　This ridiculous scene only takes a few seconds to create, and the image is so powerful that whenever you come across the words 'The Warm-up' from now on,

- first, the scene flashes into your mind;
- that will trigger the sentence, 'We All Tremble About Terribly Cold Giraffes to Feed';
- from there you write down the letters, 'W, A, T, A, T, C, G, T, F';
- and then simply reconstitute the nine key words: Water, Affirmations, Turn-ons, Acupoints, Tension easers, Concert, Goal, Time, and Fast-forwarding.

Your turn

Make mnemonic sentences for these key words. Perhaps you can make them relate to the chapter titles in some way.

13　Reading Strategies

OVERVIEW	O _____
INDEXED essays	I _____
MODELLING	M _____
More READING tricks	R _____

14　Einstein and Beyond

ELEMENTAL learning	E _____
EMBODIMENT	E _____

15　Your Preferred Learning Mode

AUDITORY, VISUAL or	A _____
KINESTHETIC	V _____
	K _____
FAST learning	F _____
HEAVY slogging	H _____
TUTORIALS	T _____
SPELLING	S _____

16　Natty Notes

ORGANIC notes	O _____
SUBLIMINAL learning	S _____
Easy ESSAYS	E _____
CREATIVE writing	C _____
MNEMONICS	M _____

Easier essays

You learned how to get information for indexed essays in Chapter 13. Natty noting is a bonus for these. Have a number of blank sheets ready. On one blank sheet list the author, title, publisher, and place and date of publication for every book you use in the essay. Give each book a sequential number for cross reference from your notes. (The idea is to record the details of the books in any convenient order at first. Later they can be put into alphabetical order.) On each of the other blank sheets you write a key phrase in the centre and write down the information you have discovered in each book (remember to add the cross-reference number) which is pertinent to each key phrase of the essay topic. Your essay is almost written for you at this point. What you do now is:

1   Pick a controversial or unusual point from one sheet with which to begin the essay. Then continue by linking up the other pieces of information you have remaining on that sheet.

2   Arrange all the other sheets in the order you prefer, using linking words such as:
    (a) Words adding to the argument—besides, above all, in addition, moreover, not only . . . but also, similarly, furthermore, later, then, also, as well, likewise, indeed, not surprisingly, etc.
    (b) Words opposing the argument—on the other hand, on the contrary, surprisingly, none the less, still, instead, although, however, nevertheless, while, though, rather, etc.
    (c) Words indicating a result of the argument—therefore, thus, thence, of course, obviously, clearly, this led to, consequently, as a result, etc.
    (d) Words illustrating the argument—for example, for instance, specifically, in particular, accordingly, for this reason, in fact, otherwise, etc.
    (e) Words summarizing the argument—in short, in conclusion, in summary, to sum up, in the final analysis, overall, on balance, it has been shown that, etc.

3   Draw the essay together using words from 2(e), then conclude by stating your own opinion based on the information you have used throughout the essay.

Creative writing

As well as taking notes from lectures (organic notes) and from books (for indexed essays), natty notes are great for any kind of creative writing, from planning a talk to your class to writing a short story or writing a personal letter.

Suppose you want to write a letter to your mother, and you cannot think of what to say after 'Dear Mum'. Here is the solution.

1   Write 'Mum' in the centre of a blank sheet.

2   Get a picture of Mum in your mind's eye, and ask her what she would like to know about. Whatever comes into your mind, write it down immediately. Ask her what else she would like to know, and write this down too. Ask her again, and write it down, and so on. Go for main ideas, rapid fire, one after the other. The quicker you do it, the better it works.

   This is the creative stage, so write down any impression you get, even if it seems silly or irrelevant. Avoid being critical with yourself, because this will dampen creativity and stop the flow. When you have plenty of ideas, go through and cross out the bits that are unsuitable. Then start writing.

Dear Mum,
Sorry it's been so long since I last wrote. The weather has been wonderful and we've been spending so much time out of doors I feel too exhausted to write when we get home late in the evening, blah, blah, blah . . .

Use the same principles for any creative writing assignment, no matter how large. Getting stuck in these is a thing of the past with natty notes. And those letters are a breeze—you can zip them off between lectures and relieve the guilt in a few minutes.

Your turn again

Turn a sheet of blank paper lengthwise. Write 'Superstudy Warm-up' in the middle, and make brief organic notes of the reviews of Chapters 1–11.

Take another sheet, and make organic notes as you read the rest of this book, using various colours. Stick them to the wall when you have finished. This way you will not have to reread the book to have all the techniques at your fingertips.

REVIEW

1 Organic notes
Get a concertina file.
Use blank sheets sideways.
Write the topic in the centre.
Write sub-topics near the topic, and write the notes towards the edge of the page.
Use simple illustrations and different colours.
Draw a leafy border around the branches when each page is finished.
Stick your notes on your wall for a week for subliminal learning.
Review your notes after one month by summarizing them into linear (normal) form.
Review both your organic notes and your linear notes before the exam.

2 Subliminal learning
Stick your notes on the wall for peripheral perception.

3 Mnemonics
List key words.
Make a ridiculous sentence using the initials of the key words.
Relate the sentence to the topic, if possible.
Use multi-sensory imagery to vivify the sentence.
Retrieve the key words by recalling the sentence.

4 Essays
Write a key word from the essay topic onto each blank sheet of paper.
Record relevant information onto each blank sheet.
Sort out the order you want for your essay.
Write it following the style for indexed essays.

5   Creative writing

Write the main idea in the centre of the page.

Ask the topic what it wants to know or tell.

Write down quickly and uncritically around the topic whatever comes to mind, no matter how silly or seemingly irrelevant.

When you have plenty to write about, cross out the notes that are unsuitable.

---

17 Your Study Environment

Furniture

If you do not yet have your own desk or table, look around the department stores or used furniture marts and buy one. 'Try before you buy' at the shop by sitting at the desk, and making sure it is the right height for you. A matt surface will prevent the problem of reflected glare, or you can use a table-cloth to cover any surface. If the top is real or imitation wood it is better to have the grain running horizontally across your field of vision when you are seated—a vertical grain in the wood tends to dissociate the left and right hemispheres of the brain. Similarly, if you use a striped tablecloth arrange the stripes horizontally. You may be able to find a desk that slopes gently up towards the rear; this is easier on the eyes and neck and sholders than a flat desk. If you have an additional desk at which you can stand up and work, you can move between the two desks and reduce any possibility of getting 'stuck' in your studying.

Use a kitchen chair or one that is firm enough to feel whether or not you are on your sitting bones.

If you have none of these niceties, fear not—nothing can prevent you from having access to all these and more in the crystal study you can generate for yourself with your developing skill in multi-sensory imagery.

Self-validation

Even with affirmative action, even though your results are improving, even though other people are admiring your progress, and even though you know you are heading in the right direction, there will still be times of self-doubt. An old saying is: 'First we get it, and then we forget it, and then we get it, and then we forget it . . .' The 'it' refers to the magnificence of the individual. Each of us catches a glimpse from time to time of our real capabilities, of the breathtaking potential every one of us has—'We get it'. And then it is gone for a while as we are submerged in the sea of poppy-cutting negativity that washes around us—'We forget it'. The more confident and able we feel, the higher we achieve, and the easier the learning seems. One way we can keep 'getting it' is by using affirmative action. Another is by continually reminding ourselves of our achievements.

Display in your room any trophies you have. Do you have any certificates for swimming or something similar? What about an object you made with your own hands? Any photos of you achieving something? Did you have a

'Letter to the Editor' published? What about photos or letters from family or friends who love you? Whatever you have, display it heroically in your room. When the down times come, this surrounding evidence will reassure you that, with all your human faults, you are still a magnificent person.

A model of excellence

One of the functions of NLP is to identify people who are excellent at what they do, and then to model them. In this sense 'to model' means to become them, to imagine you are them. By doing this, you can get closer to tapping the essence of the quality that makes them great. Using your skills of multi-sensory imagery you can play this beneficial game too.

Think of people who were famous in the subject you are studying: Marie Curie, Indira Gandhi, Maynard Keynes, etc. Read biographies of those people, or photocopy short biographies or photographs of them and stick them on the wall. Then, when it is time for you to study those subjects, take a moment to embody those people. Wrap the person around you as though you were stepping into a 'Humphrey B. Bear' outfit. Take on their personality, charisma, quirks and brilliance. Act as they would have acted, think as they would have thought, study and learn as they would have studied and learnt. Let your imagination be your guide.

Living models are useful too. Model people who are getting better results than you are. Ask them how they learn. They are usually flattered, and will happily tell you in great detail exactly how it is that they are so successful at study. When they have told you, tackle the subject their way and see what results you get. If the results are better, adopt them. If not, find another high achiever to model.

Eye-deals

If your eyes become strained through long hours of study and you seek help, beware the optician who wants to put you straight into glasses or into stronger ones—unless there are medical reasons to do so. Glasses weaken the eyes. Natural alternatives exist, and there are books of vision exercises that will show you how best to care for your eyes. Here are some basic measures to prevent deterioration of your eyesight.

1   Use an incandescent pearl globe of about 100 watts in your study lamp. Have it behind you, shining from the side or over your shoulder. Get rid of your fluorescent lamp before it starts to give you eye fatigue.

2   Keep your eyes at least 30 centimetres from the work to reduce muscle strain.

3   'Sunbathe' your eyelids. Do this with eyes closed facing towards the sun at various times of the day for a daily total of up to ten minutes. For the first ten weeks start with one minute a day, and then add a minute every week. Sunbathing stimulates and enriches the nerve centres at the back of the eyeballs. (*Warning:* Make sure your eyes are shut when you face the sun.)

4   At the end of each study segment get up and look out through the window at something far away (a street-light or a tree). Then focus cross-eyed on the tip of your nose, and then off into the distance again. Do this a couple of times as part of your instant reward for completing each good study session.

5   Another reward to give yourself is palming. Rub your hands (palms) together to warm them up, then press them to your face with palms cupped over your eyeballs. No pressure is on the eyeballs at all. You will feel this doing your eyes good straight away as the warmth from the palms radiates into your eyes and relaxes them.

The simplest diet there is

Your body is the closest environment you have to your self. It is a barometer of mental health. If you are mentally or emotionally hurt, your body will become ill or injured to attract attention because it is warning you to take better care of yourself. When you care for yourself properly you affirm your self-worth. At the very first symptom of an illness of any sort, start to pamper yourself luxuriously and immediately if you want to avoid becoming ill.

Caring for yourself means caring for your body as a part of yourself. Correct regular exercises are those such as the ones described in the warm-up. Plenty of physical activity in any form helps to keep the body tuned. Exercise that causes sweating carries accumulated toxins out of the body, and freshens up the whole system.

Rules for nutrition are simple. To sustain lengthy periods of concentration, eat something that is unsweetened for breakfast, and at least every fourth hour after that throughout the day. Unless you know a lot about nutrition or have unusual food allergies, eat an uncooked piece of fruit or vegetable and something from each of these four food groups in descending amounts every day:

Wholegrain bread, pasta or cereal   (most)

Vegetables and fruit

Beans or meat

Dairy products   (least)

$\downarrow$

This must be the simplest diet there is, and it will get you a credit rating from your doctor and the Heart Foundation.

REVIEW

1 Furniture
Have your own desk, and a chair that allows you to sit on your sitting bones.

2 Self-validation
Display evidence of your achievements in your study area.

3 Models of excellence
Find people famous in your subject areas.

Become them while you are studying.

4 Eye-deals
Use a strong non-fluorescent desk lamp.

Keep at least 30 centimetres away from your work.

'Sunbathe' your eyelids up to ten minutes daily.

Rest your eyes regularly by looking at distant objects, and by palming.

5 Nutrition
Avoid illness by having sufficient rest, exercise, and a varied diet of wholegrain foods, fresh fruit and vegetables, protein, and a little dairy food.

18 The Learning Session

Chapter 12 reviewed and recapitulated the warm-up session. Chapter 18 does the same for the strategies for the Learning Session. You already know the following twelve points, and as you read through them imagine how you could fit them into your current personal study programme.

Using the strategies

1 Overview

   After the warm-up exercises, start your learning session with a one-minute overview of the work you intend to cover during the session. This engages your right hemisphere in the learning task as well as the left.

2 Essays

   List enough books in your bibliography to make the essay respectable. Find them through the index technique. Use natty notes to collect relevant information on all the key words and sub-topics, and to sort them into writing order. Start the essay with a surprise, and end with a personal view.

3 Reading

   When time is short, read the first and last segments only. Turning headings into questions fixes your concentration. Doubling-up helps unravel tough texts. Relaxing to classical music such as that played on ABC–FM, or available on 'Superlearning' tapes, enhances concentration.

4 Embodiment

   Use the intelligence of your body and give your brain a rest. If you are bedridden, or studying in a public place, imagine multi-sensately that you are learning with your body. Einstein did it for his brilliant work, and so can you.

5 Preferred modes

   For fast learning use your preferred mode more than the other modes. For intensive learning use the three main modes—visual, auditory and kinesthetic (and add tastes and smells where possible). Respect your audience when you are giving a presentation by delivering the material in the three modes.

6   Spelling

Take a mental snapshot of troublesome words. Spelling is a visual process.

7   Natty notes

On a blank sheet turned lengthwise, write from the centre outwards, starting with the topic, then the sub-topic and any notes. Illustrate, and use colour to engage the right hemisphere. In creative writing ask your topic what it wants to say or know, and uncritically write down all that comes to you.

8   Subliminal learning

Stick your organic notes, etc., on your study wall. Experiment by playing your concert tape on your Walkman while you commute or do domestic jobs.

9   Mnemonics

Extract key words. Use their initials to make a nonsense sentence, and enliven it with multi-sensory imagery.

10   Environment

Make your study area visually appealing and reaffirming. Play gentle classical music softly in the background for a pleasant auditory environment. Use a chair and desk that help your body to maintain the correct posture for long periods of study. Look after your eyes.

11   Nutrition

Eat something raw, and something from each of the four food groups, every day.

12   Concert

At the end of the learning session record the important parts onto a cassette tape for your concert, as described in Chapter 11.

Preview

Though your learning session is complete, there is one more activity that is well worth the 60 seconds that it takes. It is to preview or scan through the topics you anticipate you are going to encounter tomorrow. Simply reading through the headings of your textbook is enough. It will help your right hemisphere participate in learning the future lesson.

Take-off time

Check your basic luggage. Tick the things you already have:

The use of two cassette recorders	☐
A blank cassette tape for each subject	☐
A variety of gentle, relaxing music	☐
Blank paper for natty notes	☐
A radio for ABC–FM	☐

A concertina file for revision ☐
A 60-minute timer ☐

Taking control

Flying requires a few preliminaries. First, passengers check in their luggage, then they board the plane. It taxies for a short while, and finally it takes off. The passengers are off, flying at supersonic speed.

When you fly with SST (Superstudy Techniques), you go through the same stages: you check your 'luggage', and board the aircraft. This stage correlates to any of the techniques in this book that you are currently using in your study. Write them down.

I am already using the following techniques:

1 _____
2 _____
3 _____
4 _____
5 _____
6 _____
7 _____

The next stage is when your aircraft starts to taxi. This is where you choose to introduce the elements of SST that are easiest to incorporate into your study schedule.

These are easy for me to introduce now:

1 _____
2 _____
3 _____
4 _____
5 _____
6 _____
7 _____

Finally the full-power take-off is when all engines are opened to full throttle, and rapidly achieve supersonic speed. This is where you take up the challenge of the remaining techniques.

I will introduce these challenging aspects as soon as I can:

1 _____

2 _____

3 _____

4 _____

5 _____

6 _____

7 _____

Trimming your SST

Even sophisticated aircraft cannot fly themselves. They need crew to plot the course, to continually evaluate progress along the flight path, to care for the passengers, and to trim or adjust the controls from time to time.

You are the whole crew of your study techniques. Only you can plot your true course. Only you can care for yourself ultimately. Only you can make the adjustments. The best crew is a pragmatic one, so use whatever works for you from this book. If something does not work, jettison it. If you become aware of even newer study technology, use it and evaluate it yourself for your own specific purposes.

Enjoy your *Superstudy* travels!

REVIEW

1 Learning techniques are summarized.

2 Preview the next day's lessons for a minute each, and they will be easier to understand.

3 Acquire the necessary equipment and stationery for your SST implementation.

4 From the *Superstudy* book identify:
   - what you are already doing,
   - what is easy to introduce,
   - what you will introduce a little later.

5 After using *Superstudy* for a while, refine it. What can you change to make it better for your own personal study routine?